CW01023662

UNDISCOVERED MINDS

Edited by

Heather Killingray

First published in Great Britain in 2002 by
POETRY NOW
Remus House,
Coltsfoot Drive,
Peterborough, PE2 9JX
Telephone (01733) 898101
Fax (01733) 313524

All Rights Reserved

Copyright Contributors 2002

HB ISBN 0 75434 393 6
SB ISBN 0 75434 394 4

FOREWORD

Although we are a nation of poets we are accused of not reading poetry, or buying poetry books. After many years of listening to the incessant gripes of poetry publishers, I can only assume that the books they publish, in general, are books that most people do not want to read.

Poetry should not be obscure, introverted, and as cryptic as a crossword puzzle: it is the poet's duty to reach out and embrace the world.

The world owes the poet nothing and we should not be expected to dig and delve into a rambling discourse searching for some inner meaning.

The reason we write poetry (and almost all of us do) is because we want to communicate: an ideal; an idea; or a specific feeling. Poetry is as essential in communication, as a letter; a radio; a telephone, and the main criterion for selecting the poems in this anthology is very simple: they communicate.

CONTENTS

LOVERS' ROCK

When I take my breath
I fall against Lovers' Rock
My unconsciousness sends me adrift
Where subconscious meets
Dazed with my desire for such a dream as this
I had never been fortunate to acquire
Alphabetically ordered emotions fall upon me
Exciting is unpredictable, and words fail to part my lips
Just a speechless sigh.
I am still drifting in the kingdom of Heaven
And faith supports me, I can go higher
But tears would pour from my heart.
I could weep for years and make no sense
Even with my lovers rock, I could frown
And pity upon my soul.
When I see and live a dream as this
Reality bites me with fangs, and blood sheds
As real as scars I have this beauty and love
But still I weep in wonder
And wonder why . . .
I still deny my lovers rock.

Helen Bulford

THE LAST POST

This is the last post,
The last mail post,
We will meet again
Sometime, somewhere
Somehow?
The love, the dreams.
The aspirations but the prison walls,
The crushing pain and the cracking,
Shattering glass.
It breaks and cracks and crashes.
Piecing peace to glass, glass to glass,
The operation, the pain-staking operation.

But suddenly the hope resolved.
Peace time,
Glass to glass?
So is this the last post?
The end and the new beginning
To die is to fail but to live
And to go into battle
Is to see the future,
Friends and the past resolved.

Wendy Chaffer

FIFTEEN FLIGHTS OF STEPS

It's been a long time since
the rainbow's end, ended here
and we dragged its pot of gold
up fifteen flights of steps
to your flat.

I sometimes wonder if we'd have
been better to split it two ways
at the bottom, and
kept our Macs on while
tossing it in separate fountains.

Peter Asher

To Belong

For though I am not owned by any persons
I have made myself a slave to all
That I may belong to the most persons
And so to the pitiable and most destitute
I became as penurious
To those mourning I have become like them
Though not a mourner myself
To delicate, I became delicate
That I might entice them to me
To affluent, I became as moneyed
Though I myself am not rich
To the kindly I have been forced to enact in such a way
Though I am not selfsame
And so to the gleeful I have become likewise,
To the ones in love I myself have become
A lovelorn and have shared with them sentiments
So I might belong I have become all things
To all people of all brands
To form a togetherness
But I have become all things
So I might provide assurance of devotion
And because of the love that's in me
I have wanted to become
A sharer of it with others
To become is what I have to be
To bring out the whole person in me
Though enroute my heart becomes a wounded pump
Nevertheless the ooze, the bruises
I have found elation in becoming.

Roseline T Chirape

LIQUID SOLUTION

Morning sun burns through the thin curtain
to reveal the state of his room.
The glass broken on the floor,
bottles strewn.
His head, the pain pushes him,
back to the pillow.
How many times he's tried,
this liquid solution
to try and dissolve his fears.
A fool and his drink are
not so easily removed.
Pain in his head, becomes
pain in his neck,
as the problems return.
He reaches out and dives back in.

Nigel J Mason

PEN PALS

Perhaps we can meet sometime
Have a real laugh
Learn to sing together
Share all our thoughts and dreams;
High vaccine
It might feel like it's illegal but it's not.

We could travel, visit places we've never seen
Let's do it, let's take a risk
So what are we waiting for?
Let's gulp down the vintage bottle of adrenaline.

It's no exaggeration to say
That happiness is short lived
So let's burn the candle at both ends
Let's make the most of it
Ride on top of the wave.

Vanity medicine taken, let's meet up.

V Topp

ROOKERY

A city of rooks
gossip in the chestnut trees.
Has something died,
and do they wait
like relatives
for the pickings of the dead?
Invisible commotions
drive them to the sky
like mud stirred at the bottom of a pool.
Black speckles underneath the clouds,
an Egyptian curse
rioting above us.
New populations
spread the city out
to other trees,
black-leafed trees
silent and ominous.
The sun discovers a blue sheen
the quietness becomes a raucous threat
against our timid, superstitious minds.

Fred Brown

STANLEY AND RITA

(Celebration of fifty golden years of marriage)

Dear Rita

Happy anniversary - fifty years of life, love, happiness,
and tears - all with me.

Honey, we did it. We climbed to the top of the mountain
and slid down the other side of it.
And the two of our most important treasures are our daughters -
Karen and Julie - we love them without measure.
We worried and fussed and worried some more -
Especially when the boys started to come thru' the door.
You know we tried our best to instil traditional family values
for the girls to follow in their lives.

Well honey, we finally made it! I congratulate and love you -
Love Stanley

Dear Stanley

My love, my life I have loved being your wife for fifty years.
Though water may freeze in the cold and the window of our life
may have melted at times in life's heat.
But, in my contentment I still know and feel my first love for you
with a peaceful bliss.

I congratulate and love you on our 50th wedding anniversary.
Love Rita

Colin Zarhett

HELL CAN BE REVISITED MANY TIMES ON THIS EARTH

Be it the child suffering in silence from the pain and hurt caused by an adult or another child, it became too great to bear, so a hidden world is invented, a haven away from the living hell, where in an imagination not yet blinded and stunted by years of growing up, can freely roam, where love can be given unconditionally and is limitless.

Hell can be revisited many times on this earth

A nation suffering as a multitude, when the long awaited rains still have not fallen or civil war rages, bringing destruction to all in its path. Hunger becomes a disease, a basic human necessity denied and death a way of life.

Hell can be revisited many times on this earth

The man, woman or child trapped in a way of life due to circumstances beyond their control, where the sale of pleasure ensures their survival and in some cases that of their families.

Hell can be revisited many times on this earth

Then there are those that live in constant fear, because of political religious beliefs, sexual preferences or purely because of the colour of their skins. They are persued, hunted and trapped, in most cases because of inherited prejudices and fears.

Hell can be revisited many times on this earth

There are incurable sicknesses that takes hold of the human body and mind, wrecking the fibres of its works, where medication is administered to relieve pain but only leads to prolonging the suffering.

Hell can be revisited many times on this earth

Robertine Muriel

UNFINISHED BUSINESS

Sometime, I'll come to Kismet
And I'll say, 'Kismet,
We have unfinished business
You and I.
Reticence only serves to magnify
The distant pain of parting, and
Quicken a present grief.'
If I know Kismet
She will make me cringe,
Tongue like a whip, she'll say,
'Never a word for three decades
Of days,
Sets quite a new dimension
On your funny little ways.
Now you're expecting
That I'll rouse my limbs
And dance attendance on your
Precious literary whims.'
But I know Kismet.
If she sees me cringe
Her eyes will soften
Under her comely fringe
And if she listens
To my tale of woe, she'll
Whisper that she thought
About me so.
And if she hears me cry,
She'll say,
'We have unfinished business
You and I.'

Dean Juniper

NURSERY

So this battleship linoleumed room
with its sensible chimney piece
where once the fender stood,
was your nursery,
little flaxen-haired dreamer?
Was your own battleship
in the safety of whose doorway
you did daily battle
with a household full of giant tyrants,
'til, door slammed, you discarded
your public mask of timidity
and dreamed great dreams.
This where you sat at your knee-high table
studiously dividing your green pastille
between the china plates of your three dolls -
equal portions for all.
This where you fought great fears
as the night-time shadows loomed
in the light of your bedtime candle
and wolves behind the door
merged with your troubled dreams;
until dawn woke you with
the raucous cries of rooks.
And where you weathered the storms,
your dream-world your protection.
What fairy haven beckoned you then?
And have you at last
reached out for that magic place
and found it - deep within?

Stella Durand

SNATCH-MOMENTS

Snatch-moments,
happy, happy times,
robbed within a lousy day
that's brimming with frustrations,
all cluttered full of haste and waste.

Snatch-moments,
airy seconds far too brief,
pick-pocketed and hustled
from the bustle of our lives.
Little cameo rushes,
tail ends we film and grab
in spite of time.
We catch them in an updraft
with downstretched palms,
fingering those carefree wisps
like lazy locks of hair.

Snatch-moments,
strobed spurts of bliss.
Here in a flash, gone even quicker.
No signposts, no diary
to tell us when and where they'll come.
Hiccups of some kindly fate
that pities us
in error or in vain.

Snatch-moments,
why not grab them when we can?
Sunny spasms
before the clouds roll in.
A smiling face
between disgruntled looks.
A heady rose
when all around exhausts exhaust.
A warm caress
where none's expected.

Snatch-moments,
millisecond joys.
If you miss them . . .
Tough!

René James Hérail

No Future In The Past

Is old age but a think-in maudlin' visual,
just to search out fondest memories in our mind
whilst we slip-slide slowly from life's shovel
to join in death as manure of a kind?
- a final sadness numbing all ambition
with longing for past life, a soulful gaze
denying in unseemly contradiction
useful purpose for so many used up days?
We could perhaps with faith discount such theory
and forwards glance to life beyond the grave
so that reflection might not make us weary
nor pending death require us to be brave.
And if rheumatic body ail us
and guide creak-kneed ascent of stair
we still have mind to exercise and nourish
which age alone can't necessarily impair.
So let us save 'hereafter' for reflection
and for the past shed not a single tear
but presently with thought attempt perfection
and see perhaps life's meaning crystal clear.

W Ballantyne Scott

FOOT PASSENGER

Go my love, do what you do
if he could love you as I do
if he could take your hand
for a walk along the sand
when I miss you
eyes brimming with tears
if he could weep like child
who needs mother's breast
even has much money
he couldn't smell a rose
or to defer between thorn and flower
what kind of woman are you
got to learn who is the real poor
have you ever been in school?
Or passing your time
near your swimming pool
getting sunburnt?
You liked always to be cool.

Hacene Rahmouni

DROWNING

Drowning under waves of darkness
I hide away upstairs in my room:
door shut
windows shut
curtains drawn
you lose track of time
you feel you are going
out of your mind
awful melancholy
sapping my energy
eroding my will to live
you feel you have nothing to give
drowning under dark waves
these savage seas seek to sink
the suffering spirit
these seas seethe
with grief
I find no relief
I try to sleep
find, I cannot weep
no point counting sheep
as I drown under waves
think of my grave
find I cannot pray
and cannot face the day
I strive to survive
this mental storm
occasionally wish
I'd never been born
confused and torn
vulnerable and unwell
because of this living hell.

Alex Warner

PERCEPTION

Alone, a goddess stands,
And spins.
Slowly turning,
Rotating. Gyrating.

Faster now she spins.
Earth is turning,
Whirling. Twirling,
Onwards.

Ever onwards, round it spins.
Is she the culmination of all life?
A central pillar?
Or an elm tree in a gale?

For, now my turning stills
And I become just one more
Speck
On the Earth's horizon.

Rebecca Murphy (13)

WISPS OF MEMORY

Beneath lay the islands

lands of,

> legendary raiders
> Orkneyingasaga
> mainland settlers

the engines loud roar, invited reverie

I sank, memory deep, to become,

the child I had been . . .

> freewheeling giddily
> curved country roads
legs dangling

> bounding purpled heath
feet squelching

> leaping burns, flecked amber
splashing cold

> sailing Mistress Scapa
scudding her slate-grey waves
> as Arctic terns soared
and curlews dipped

> exploring tiny sheep filled isles
> seals bobbing and basking
sharing pebbled shore

> gazing the Old Man's craggy brow
staring seawards . . .

Memory wisps of Hoy
paradise playground

fasten seat belts
touchdown

Forty years I dreamt return
heard the Islands' call

Now Kirkwall's ancient streets
I walked anew
Saint Magnus towered, red, vain glorious
lilting voices spoke soft, welcome

Happiness churned.

June Fox

A BUDDING CYCLE

Life is like that of a rose,
Fresh when still a bud
Each petal flourishing as time passes by
Opening its mind to the new world around it
Oblivious to the dangers unseen
Slowly but surely
The trouble seeps in
Like the wind and the rain
Uncontrollably jealous of this bloom's novelty
Whose delicate eyes begin to open
Whose innocent mind begins to stir.

Life is like that of a thorn,
Whose sharp mind is
The ugly appearance
And sharp stinging ambitions
Seeking the opportunity
To destroy the buds around it
To conquer their minds
The poison of this devil's sword
Begins to seep into the buds
Weakening strength
Arising problems
Awakening the nightmares.

Life is like that of light,
Concealed by clouds
But rays shining through.
For a dozen hours a cloth masking its very existence
For a dozen or more its radiance showing.
Surrounded by thorns of the sky
Yet never fading
Never failing
Never falling
The troubles discarded
No nightmares seep in.

A mind full of determination
Determined to be bright
Eyes opening to beauty
Flouting the thorns
Displaying the magnificence.
The charisma will show
Like that of a rose.

Karishma Brahmbhatt

MY TWENTY PENCE PIECE

You hid inside the darkness, a part of me
I never got a chance to pass you on to another, the light,
Quick was your journey through my outer layer
Arriving in a land of which you could never leave.

Every day I greeted you
Your circles and pentagons kept me sane
I needed you, others envied me
They tried to recreate your glory and failed
Only I could spin you.

Soon your layer of protection wore thin
I had relied on you one time too many
I could see through your grey wall to the silver beneath
It was almost time for us to part company
For you improve the sanity of another.

So I let you leave me, no longer needing you
Perhaps you are still there
Maybe you're back in circulation
I'll never know
I moved on and left that world behind me.

Lynsey Stopforth

VILLAGE TWILIGHT HAYDON BRIDGE

On reaching the old stone bridge
In the golden atmosphere of the evening
Before the night fell into the river
And the river held its breath
Before tumbling over the weir,
I saw a silvery pool bubbling away
Alive with eels, all squirming and wriggling.

I felt the rhythm of the water
Beat into me, dark, mysterious, inviting.
Fascinated, I stood and watched until diverted
By a loud splash behind me.
Not a salmon but a perch, someone said,
But I would like to think it was a salmon
Here from far, far away.

The nightly flight of crows
Swept overhead following the river west
Towards Ridley Hall and Allen Bank.
Soon the lights, plucked from the Anchor,
Were playfully twinkling on the water,
Rippling, dancing, absorbing the shadows
As the sun sank into the gathering dusk.

An in-between silence followed
But not for long. The spell was rudely broken.
Something had disturbed the geese and ducks
On the far side of the river, soon followed
By the haze-wrapped swarms of midges
And as the street lights appeared
The last of the quiet Northern daylight vanished.

Myra Bowen

UNDERGROUND BED

Why do men destroy creation of mankind
With weapons of mass destruction;
As if men are not of the same kind:
Who are not entitled to restitution?

To send men to untimely grave
Is perilous; a consequence very grave
When men make underground bed
For feeble foes.
Let them honour the underground bed
With their kith and kin.

The painter paints out rays
Of beauty all the days
Of his life.
He thinks out the ways
Of excellent beauty all nights of his life.
The artist constructs the semblance
Of nature's image with assemblance
Of images and brain cognisance
Giving us appreciable adorable
And semblance of adoration.

The sculptor reconstructs man's heart
To give us natural balance
According to his perception
According to his appreciation
Acceding to his creation
So that man reminds
Himself of the past
Present and future-past
As a mark of assertion.

The physician belabours to attend to the wounded;
Nurses scamper to clean their wounds;
The teacher imparts knowledge.
Society is encouraged to acknowledge;
Virtue of service to mankind.

What does the weapons
Of mass destruction do?
For who are guns for?
Let the maker test the semblance,
The appreciation of his work
With his kith and kin.
So that he can adore the creativity of
Creating skeletons in underground bed.

Abraham Ekeoma O

YOU NEVER KNOW

You never know what troubles people have
Never know exactly what's on their mind
They can smile, look happy, even friendly
But you never know what's on their mind
What troubles pervade their inner being
What kind of hole they are struggling to get out of

You never know of the frustrations people fight with
The uncertainties they carry along with them
They can become adept at putting on a brave face
But you never know what sucks at their life force
Robbing them of a happier life
Keeping contentment at arm's length

We never know what lessons we have to learn
What sort of difficulties will stop us in our tracks
Never can tell when we sympathise with others
How long it will be before we're treading the same path
It has been said that we're never given more than
we can cope with
So cope well, learn the lesson and benefit from the
tribulations that are yours.

Valerie Thorley

A MOMENT OF ESCAPISM

Four grey walls a prison make,
But let your mind awander,
Away from locks and bars and things,
Lots of things much grander.

Let it be a garden green,
With flowers full of brightness,
A shining sun with blue, blue skies,
Such a thing is sightless.

There's girls and boys to play with,
To laugh and joke and toy,
To make your life more pleasant,
To fill you full of joy.

There's joyous calming music,
Then a loud, loud bell!
'It's dinner time,' the warden shouts,
You see a flat grey wall.

Angela Helen

REFLECTIONS

Magic mirror on the wall
We look in you to see it all
What you keep from those that view
What is it we see in you
Is that me or is that you?

I move, you move, you see me,
Down into your heart to peer and look
At pages in your picture book
To see the truth for those that try
To look into your glass so wise.

The truth that hides within our souls
The love, the hate, the worry folds
The smile that turns the face aglow
The light that shines in eyes so bright
That turns dark days to brightest night.

Magic mirror on the wall
How many times have you seen all?
The pictures you have stored inside
A million views of parts of time
When you have looked from high above
And seen the face of hate and love.

On and on your film runs on
No dark room for the camera man
No chemist shop to take the film
No fee, no charge, you give it all
The picture free from on your wall.

Sweet mirror, thank you for your gifts so free
Like apples on an orchard tree.
To give a picture is for you
A second in a field of view
To us a moment in our lives
When we can gaze into your eyes
To see how life has treated us
And how to look for those to trust.

Magic mirror on the wall
Gleam and shine your glass to all
To all who look and gaze at you
To find the picture of the truth
The heart and soul in each of us
That needs to reach for love and trust!

T R Tully

A Song For Charlotte

Asleep in beauty, awake in peace
My head finds rest at your breast as I sleep
Sleeping softly, our hearts keeping time
With each beat, each motion a symphony of rhyme

You lie dreaming, your breath, like cool waters lapping the shore
Your heartbeat so gentle, tranquil, absent of war
No tossing or turning, on our bed this tiny ship's deck
No storms or disturbance, no arid wasteland shipwreck

Tell me your secrets, tell me your tales
Of your journey this far, through the wind and the rain
Shipwreck, disaster, liberation or fear
Maybe it was these things that brought you to me

And now you're here, I hope you'll stay
Not discontent, distracted by the beauty of lands far away
Our chariot awaits, led by the white horses of the sea
In a flowing white dress with my vow on your finger in a dream.

Oliver R Howells

CONTRARIWISE

Earnings and spendings are said
to measure work,
snores and excuses clearly
measure shirk.
Those that have work
sometimes scorn it,
those that lack it
always mourn it:
this undoubted contradiction
leads to friction.
Smiling, the Creator looks on from afar -
'Ah well,' he says, 'ah well, that is how people are.'

Margaret Roach

A STEP FROM TIME

Soft grey mist drifting in the vales,
Billowing tatters of forgotten dreams.
A floating shroud to soften ugly scars,
Man's legacy from passing years.

Sunbeams reaching from the sky,
Midas touch turns mist to sea of gold.
The years recede and time stands still
As beauty holds me fast within its spell

Too soon, the clouds obscure the sun,
Magic fades, reality comes flooding back.
Yet, the memory of that magic will live on,
A step from time into a land of dreams.

Florence Hall

FOGLANDER

His rubber-soled feet creep up behind you,
grey tracksuit top and bottom drags you down,
the sounds grabbed from your throat by this mugger,
blurred focus on an unfamiliar street.

Try telling yourself he's just leftover,
congealed, not fit for Goldilocks' porridge, as
he rises from the drains, all stage-smoke,
shaking beads of moisture from stovepipe hat -

one of a thousand faces already
dissolving - plunging you back in a
blanched Underworld. Now he's the ferryman
embarking an unwilling spirit across
some nowhere threshold of oblivion,
his silver coin swallowed, you, part of him.

Brian Garfield

REMEMBRANCE DAY

They did not know as they waited alone,
Whether their loved ones would ever come home.
As they gazed through the window out in the night.
Criss-cross with white beams of the searchlight.
They did not know as they heard aircrafts' drone,
Whether their loved ones would ever come home.
The loud thud of bombs as they fell in the night,
And fire and the sparks, a terrible sight.
The shattered plane fell like a stone,
Was it a loved one who would not come home?
What price must they pay in a world full of strife,
The ultimate one, the cost of a life.
In countries afar in a man-made hell,
They didn't come back, they lay where they fell.
And for those who waited at home all alone,
Would it be their loved one who would not come home?
They will always be remembered!

Ivor Emlyn Percival

UNTITLED

You can tell me that you love me
    a thousand times a day
and show me in every possible way,
but only when I see it in your eyes
    do I know that it can't possibly be lies.

Sheri-lynne Dike Johns

PLAYING MY GAME

My dad made a hundred, how far have you got?
Watch that ball, strike hard when it's hot
If I had the courage, in the end to wonder
Since most of what happens, is not planned at all
Who is to say, what's going to be,
Is the morrow, as yesterday, to be, no less, for me?
Not so, each day so different
Wayward clouds, roll destroy and refashion
Earthy forms phan'tom bits and pieces
Tomorrow, not known how you played,
Or the score, the umpire's finger, says, no more
When the bails fly, another to bat
Tomorrow is someone's first day
One out, one in, your last day, his first
Not as I was, when part of my fold
The birds from my nest have flown, got old
An earlier time, had me in place
Counting the hours, part of the race
86 summers, gone, to some place,
From nowhere to somewhere
We all play the game, and win what
We exist to play, to make such as me
With no plan in sight, having to fight
Who cares, to say well done
Am I so different, from anyone?
No trace, forgotten, gone,
Unknown, how well we played
How far we got, brawn not wanted
To increase the fold, play the game
Increase the fold, what's new to being old
Grandad was in the family team,
His name Dimn, and what he went through
He played the game, thought as you
Do the things that count,
Try to think what all is about.

Someday, one may say Grandad did that,
'Tis my turn to bat
He made 100, I have not made a lot
Hit the ball hard, 'tis all you've got,
They'll remember a six
Before a howzat.

H Cotterill

PRESTIDIGITATION

Eight fingers and two misshapen Slavic thumbs
belonged to Grandma's hands.
Not one was comely
though God bequeathed each one a magic power.
Once, long ago they'd poked and picked and tickled
shoved foes, pushed buttons, pointed
drummed youth's exasperation
and later, brightly decked with painted fingernails
and golden rings, they'd held pencils, paint brushes
and pens, sewed intricate seams but
eventually they learned new arts;
shelling lima beans, changing diapers, wiping tears
patting heads, chopping carrots, beckoning, soothing
sculpting the green clay of other hands
small and dimpled, until those too
had grown capable and confident.
Assiduously, her skilful fingers sustained
everything they'd ever touched or held:
then, at just the proper interval
with dignified reluctance . . . they let go.

Carol D Glover

WARMTH OF SUMMER

Shall I compare thee
To the warmth of summer rain
Apart from getting drenched
And running down the drain
I feel that warmth
Falls on me
Coming out of clouds
Although I am often getting wet
Am feeling rather proud
Especially through warmth
Warmth of, yes, the sun
So not really miserable
But feel a sense of fun.

M D Bedford

THE DREAM

I could almost feel the silence
Vibrating all around
I could smell the subtle fragrance
Of the flower strewn ground
I could see the true perfection
Of a real summer day
As I walked in that procession
Slowly along my way.

The climb was long and winding, and
Suspended from the skies
Was a pure white cloud that curtained
The summit from my eyes.
Disappointment and frustration
I fought to keep at bay
As I walked in that procession
Slowly along my way.

My companions were strangers
Yet I felt we were friends
And together through all dangers
We'd struggle to the end
Overwhelmed by our emotions
We knew no words to say
As I walked in that procession
Slowly along my way.

The quickening of our pulses -
Excitement spurred us on
As hundreds of joyful faces
Greeted our happy throng.
I saw dear friends and relations
The welcome was so gay
As I walked in that procession
Slowly along my way.

Then the white mist swirled around me
Lost in the encircling cloud
I cried, 'Wait, oh please don't leave me,'
And sank down to the ground.
How had I earned this desertion
What mistake had I made?
As I walked in that procession
Slowly along my way.

How long was I unconscious
Before the throbbing pain
Brought me slowly to vicious
Reality again?
Gone is the anticipation
The perfect summer day
As I walked in that procession
Slowly along my way.

A grave face comes close to me
A kind hand holds my own
And strangers once again I see
But happiness is gone.
Sympathy, consideration,
Replace those feelings gay
As I walked in that procession
Slowly along my way.

Puzzled - my thoughts I try to clear
'Where am I?' I implore.
'You're safe among friends now, my dear
But you were at death's door.'
Overcoming my confusion
I remember that day
As I walked in that procession
Slowly along my way.

Jennifer Butler

NOT SUCH A BAD DAY

Sat, curved around me,
I sat wrapped in this feeling
of a little-known butter yellow blanket.

Out, hidden smiles they came,
out of their grate
from the depths of their confinement.

Black and soft yellow don't mix -
one pushes the other clean out.

How absurd such a change can occur so fast
despite of myself
for this whole, this fleeting moment,
content, I sat, with me.

Emily Allen

A Strong Heart Will Prevail

In our minds we live
>In our dreams we die
In our hearts we give
>In our lives we try

The pain we've endured
>The promises we've made
The pity we've cured
>The prevalence we've paid

Mark Jeavons

EVERY YEAR

twenty people in India are killed by falling coconuts;
thirty-five thousand million bananas are harvested in Brazil
and scores of incredible facts are reported in in-flight magazines.

Squared off, through portholes left and right, it's hard to believe that
thirty-five thousand square kilometres of the world's forests
are being destroyed every week; there's so much down there. But;

by next week, it may be starring in a Greenpeace video,
bulldozers growling round mutilated copses, piles of chained,
limbless trunks being dragged off into smoky clearings;

a watery sun, trembling through the heat from the burning debris,
bringing a charred lump to the throat and a tear to the eye.

Every day, thirteen thousand tonnes of fish are eaten in Japan.

John Kay

WOLF MOON

Silver secrets reflect on me
Lunar comes unto my doom
Howling the depths and deep
The dark side of the moon

Receptive caller of the tides
Archangel of the darkness lay
Shields us in the solstice ties
Mystery of the night, give way

Soothing mystics waxing wane
Eons of unchallenged power
Bewitching all within its gaze
Ruler of the midnight hour

Alexa Raisbeck

Is There Anything Out There?

Why the need to be mobile eared
on the bus, in the car, in the street?
Ominous obedience to barmy
bleeping resounds.
Sinister silence to rhythms
bleeding around.
Chattering mobile mobs, too keen
to be seen using the machine.
Totally out of the scene they are in.

Why the need to turn on tea and
television with automatic submission?
Open a box to select our thoughts.
Be enthralled with what's installed.
Watch and watch, just to be involved
remotely animated, titillated, captivated
by the scene, seen on the screen.
Totally out of the scene we are in.

Why the need to wallow in a web
where discovery waits well prepared?
Ready to use it as a rule not a tool,
when whimsically we wonder what's
really out there?
Totally out of the real scene set.
Why? - Escapism is the new reality!
Conning conveniences virtual vitality
to pampered press button activists.

Rosalia Campbell Orr

MESS WITH ME

Nature enraged -
Her fury
Wrecked man's toil.
She showed her strength
And yielded power,
Destruction
Was her aim.
And man,
For all his worth,
Limped
In sadness,
Humiliated and humble,
In admission
Of his guilt -
That of greed.

Lyn Sandford

THE CHILD

The child must be our main concern
From past disasters we must learn
The child must be first, always and last
We must not repeat events of the past
The child must be part of our plans
With the child lies the survival of man

The child must be shown loving and trust
Not beaten and bruised then ground into dust
Taught how to share, taught how to give
To build a world where we all can live
We must give the child all that we can
Without the child there's no hope for man

Derrick Hopper

THE FEEL-GOOD FACTOR

There is a little lady called D Cromer of Salom Residential
Care Home in Norwich,
A haven of peace for many who live there,
It's a feel-good factor knowing it's a happy home for many.
A little lady of 101, which is an age of life which very few make it.

She has a teddy bear who she calls Charlie,
She adores her teddy bear, and cuddles it with pride and joy.
Cromer is so easy to please and always smiles, no matter what happens.
A little frail lady who likes life, and never complains about anything.
A brave lady in her own way who never stops, reminding us she is 101,
A star in her own right.

The feel-good factor is that I am going to be old
And hope I can be like her.
A little lady who never stops cuddling her bear for comfort, she is
Always happy in her own way, and looks so able in her ability
To hold a cup and does it with grace.
A good person in her own way and a friend to everyone.
A little lady happy in her life, a zest that is full of goodness,
She never has anything bad to say about anybody.
She loves food, and never says no if she is given anything.

A little lady called Cromer 'D' is a star in her own right,
The feel-good factor of a little lady, who is so happy with people
around her,
Long live Cromer 'D' of 101. May you live forever as you will never
Be forgotten by those who know you, as you will always be
Remembered for your smile, which was your way to express yourself,
A simple lady so little but big in age.

F Walls

LE MARCHÉ

I had seen a woman in the market place
her eyes were troubled . . .
She was beautiful. Her hair was starched,
her dress unkempt, yet to me
she seemed heaven sent.
I watched her haggle for provisions.
I followed her for you know what.

But what was my concept of this woman
I'd never seen.
Was it one of warmth, of compassion,
some reality, that's what I mean?

I hope I'll see her again,
I hope she'll notice me.
And turn her eyes wonderingly . . .
'Have I seen this man before?
Why does he stare so?
Oh, yes, I remember, on a Saturday, in the market place,
I saw him there.'

But he didn't beckon as death can do,
he just smiled, and we went about our business
in the market place, as we do.

A few months later, on a Saturday
I wandered down to the market place
and I saw a woman choosing vegetables
and counting every penny of their cost,
and being so much more adventurous
and so much surer of my French,
'Je dit combien.'

She threw me a furtive stare . . .
To which I replied,
'Je regret l'insinuation,'
but it can't be denied,
that I saw you, and you saw me,
in the market place, and now I'm unable to forget
or remember, if we met.

And so we met.

Our life was idyllic . . .
her face lost its lost look.
She became full of confidence and joy,
she lost her ragamuffin clothing
and replaced it with Yves St Laurent.

She became 'La Mademoiselle' of our district.

I pondered and I wondered
I searched and I realised
that sometimes it's better to leave people alone
and let them stand or fall.

And now you may say
that this poetry no longer rhymes,

that sometimes poetry doesn't rhyme,
sometimes life is just a fallacy of time.
Who can say, who can do,
who can explain reality
is it you?

Geoffrey Fletcher

Cows' Week

It's Cows' Week, it's Cows' Week!
Time to do more than just browse week.
Time to forget the production of milk,
Time to dress up with fine ribbons and silk;
Time to clean hooves of glutinous mud,
Time to do more than lie chewing the cud.

It's Cows' Week, it's Cows' Week!
To do more than the farmer allows week.
Kick up your heels and join in the fun,
Bovine festivities out in the sun.
Jerseys and Guernseys and Alderneys all
Throw off your routine and let's have a ball!

It's Cows' Week, it's Cows' Week!
Mooing (not barks or miaows) week.
Hold up your tails and throw up your horns,
Let's go and trample on somebody's lawns!
Flatten their bushes and chew up their flowers,
Really enjoy it for hours and hours.

It's Cows' Week, it's Cows' Week!
A celebration (and how) week;
And though we can't dance
We can kick up and prance
And fill up on succulent grass.
And, when we're replete, we'll find a nice street
And allow hundreds of cowpats to pass!

We'll garnish our udders and keep out of the mud as
If we were debutantes.
We will tease the old bulls
And, in the odd lulls,
We'll lead them a hell of a dance.

We'll lie under the trees and do just as we please
And look for a pasture unfenced;
We'll stop all lactation
To hell with the nation!
They'll have to make do with condensed!

Our midsummer fling is our very own thing
And if we want perms in our tails,
Then we'll have them and you
Know what you can do
You'll not take the wind from our sails!

And when the week's done
And we've all had our fun
We'll return to our pastures, I fear;
And, if they don't ill-treat us,
We'll resume giving litres
But be thinking of Cows' Week next year!

Dennis A Calow

MADONNA

Such tenderness, even in stone -
the master's soft touch,
mother and child, inseparable;
carved from the same immortal block.

But please, come closer . . .
I have to whisper, not move my lips:
I couldn't bear another miracle -
(the crowds are bad enough already)
yet I must tell someone . . .

I'm just not sure this is *me* somehow:
All this everlasting motherhood. I only seem
weighed down by it all, the awesome responsibility,
his endless questioning, the constant
fidgeting and jockeying in my lap
forcing me into saying ridiculous things like,
'You'll fall . . .'

Then of course he cocks his little head
- smiles up so disarmingly, reminding me he has his future,
those finely chiselled features
chiding my self-importance.
Turns my cheek towards him.
He knows it all already -
(I wonder if it had been a girl, would I have felt different?)

Look closely,
the cracks are clearly there: fault-lines
in the mould,
I can feel their seismic grating,
announcing his departure. No doubt
he will leave a consoling kiss on this weary forehead,
telling me not to worry - everything
will sort itself out one way or another.
And of course he'll keep in touch . . .

Oh my little one,
if nothing else remember just
one pearl of wisdom from your mother.
Be sure to have no children of your own,
or how will you ever find the time
to change the world?

Pete Mullineaux

MEMORIES

How oft' do we, when sat alone,
With silence and firelight's glow,
Recall in sentimental tone
The memories of long ago?

That day when Mother scolded you
When you came home with feet all wet.
The puddles you had trampled through
To see how dirty you could get.

The birthday bike when you were ten,
The one you'd dreamed of night and day,
And how you showed it proudly when
Your friends called in for you to play.

Those happy times on Bonfire Night,
With coloured stars and crackers gay.
The Christmas tree with fairy lights
And gifts for all on Christmas Day.

The rambles through the countryside
In spring and sunny summertime.
The tadpole pond and, close beside,
An old oak tree you used to climb.

Your first day's work - do you recall
The morning when you went to start?
How strange you felt - so shy and small,
With lump in throat and quickening heart.

And then there was your wedding day,
And your first baby daughter too.
All these things seem but yesterday.
The memories ring so clear and true.

And yet they happened long ago
Along the journey up life's lane,
And, though the years roll by, you know
These pleasant memories will remain.

And, when you're by your fireside,
Alone and, maybe, feeling blue,
They'll come to comfort and provide
The smiles to keep you smiling through.

Alan Edmundson

CUMBERLAND AN EXILE REMEMBERS

In my waking hours, in my heart and blood,
memories flow back, when past my fading vision,
zoom the car plated AOs, HHs, RMs.
Some say, Cumbrians don't travel.
But I have forsaken beloved fells,
and brooding, bewitching lakes.
The skies above Enfield, the heart is in Ennerdale.
Now it's a Stobart, in articulated splendour.
Fast Eddie's growling juggernauts,
are you bound for home? Can I follow you?
On TV the news is bearable, when you Anna,
dark beauty, make all news good news.
Even the Lord Bragg, brings to mind,
my great grandsire, and desirable Wigton.
From coast to coast, Wainwright of fond memory,
please one deviation for me, may I leave Robin Hood's Bay
and trek to Bega's bosom, for my rest?
Oh bless you Ritson and your bar, I'd never lie, about
magnificent Wasdale, or the feats of Joss Naylor.
Yes Lakeland I miss you, and long for the sight
of your peerless wrestlers, and valiant trail hounds.
And last but never least, far far away John Peel,
who I will always ken.

Eddie Fennell

THE WARRIOR'S TREASURE

Ultrasophisticated,
A true poet with dreams,
Orphaned by words divided by screams,
A genius,
Unexpected,
Giggles,
Then cry,
Despite their attempts true poets don't die,
The truth stretched,
Bring order to life,
'Eamon Healy the Warrior Poet and 'Joyce' his wife,
One day this world will realise
And his poetry will explode before your eyes,
Then your experience,
The ultimate pleasure,
The passion of poetry that's the warrior's treasure.

Rosmary Healy

TERSE VERSE

This terse verse,
Will only get worse.
I haven't a clue how to do it
I will have a go,
But you really should know,
When I'm stuck with my pen, well I chew it!
Confessions aside,
I'll conquer my pride,
And sit with my head in my hands.
When inspired again,
I will pick up the pen,
And see where the blessed thing lands.
When I was a child,
So sweet and so mild,
I was a poet and knew it.
But now comes the time,
When I've quite passed my prime,
And know for a fact that I blew it!

Elizabeth Whaley

THE GYPSY AND THE GORGIO

She danced around the campfire,
As the flames reached into the night.
It was then that he walked by,
But she knew that he wasn't right.

Maria was just a gypsy girl,
And with a gorgio she fell in love.
But he did not return her affections,
And she had no help from up above.

Desperately she turned to the Devil,
She sold her family's souls for evil things.
He turned her father into a sound box,
Her mother into a bow, four brothers into strings.

The Devil then took the six souls,
And he turned them into a violin.
Maria quickly learnt to play it well,
And the courtship of the gorgio did begin.

The gorgio fell in love with her,
But the Devil had two more souls to claim.
He took Maria and her lover to Hell,
And the violin fell to the ground, where it did remain.

A poor gypsy boy found it there,
He played constantly till he got a wife.
And ever since that fateful day,
It has been the musical symbol of gypsy life.

Robert Meader

WHY?

I stand upon this Mother Earth and wonder why this is.
I look at growth in flower and tree born of a seed and fertile soil.
I witness breeze, gale and storm, feel gratitude from an orb of gold,
and set within a darkened sky see that silver face of mirth,
and wonder, why this Birth.

I see the wheel, the flint tool work, the arrowhead and spear,
and upon that stone face marked, the animals held dear.
I have searched the sea, the plain and tree; yet find no line to me.
In natures time scale I am new, yet lot in Antiquity.

One book sets me to bog and mud, another begs I follow the beast.
The Bible recalls I am born of flesh in Adam's garden of the east,
but I am the image of Abbe the God, am a stranger to this sphere,
as the constant battle against nature attests, no harmony lies here.

Stupidity, greed and arms for blood, what is the reason I cry,
and stand upon this Mother Earth, why, why, why?

Brian Smith

THE SONG AND THE DANCE

Was it worth it? The song and the dance,
The music was fitful, but the melodies were superb.
Now it is quiet, so quiet, memory strains to hear.
Gone is the poetry, the rush of warm expression.

Silence, dull silence, the stillness of nothing.
The dancing melodies, the swirling, rushing to crescendo,
The words fall away as the dance becomes a minuet.
There *was* a song, rich and warm, perfect, so natural,
The mind and body in harmony.

More measured is the rhythm now, the tempo of a powane,
Patterned neatly with regular beat, but all excitement gone.
Was it worth it, the song and the dance?
Yes, oh yes, beautiful times, exciting moments of love and pleasure.
Of people met and the richness of their company.
Sharing their joys and sadness.
Watching tragedies relentlessly unfold, asking why and why?

Gone the mazurkas and the arias of one youth.
Now I move in the even and deeper melodic tones of the largo.
This is the song of one's maturity.

H M Pell

FAST FORWARD

We vie with weather and with clime
We try to stem the march of time
We try to manage and to cope
We're full of charms, full of hope
We've suffered the shocks and dealt with the blows
Life's never easy as everyone knows.

Childhood for some is alive, full of joy
For others a trial, be it girl, be it boy
In adulthood maybe the tables may turn.
The child who was happy may grow to ill fate
The other may travel to Heaven's own gate

Which was the case, our time is too brief.
We march with the clock without ire or relief
The end comes at last not too far from the start
We heave a great sigh, from a tired old heart
We can no longer breathe - no longer stand
There's the old man with the scythe in his hand!

Cyril Joyce

DEMOCRACY MISUSED

I'm a chap who likes to investigate
    how some organisations perform
and I find that democratically
    they never work to norm

Democracy is about the majority
    and with debates is always used
but sometimes the power of money
    causes the system to be abused

When I take in the United Nations
    I find democracy in disarray
as both Britain and America
    seems to want things all their way

They take command in everything
    whilst the majority are left out
I believe it's through their military power
    which gives them both this clout

Yet they rant on about democracy
    and on how things should be run
when in actual fact with what they do
    is to rule folk with the gun.

Lachlan Taylor

A WEE POEM FOR ALL MY FRIENDS

This world so big, so wide,
yet still I cannot find
a wee place for me to hide
to live life slow at peace,
in my soul, in my mind,
so fast this world I find.

People here move so fast
I dread they soon might crash,
expect so much out of life,
in my heart I dread and fear,
this race they try to embrace.

Yet all I desire, a wee place,
far, yet so near and good beer,
a wee quiet place to hide,
rest my head to lie and cry
to live at peace in my mind.

A wee place to walk,
to embrace slowly a pace,
I sigh my dog and I,
stand still to ponder,
just a wee bit longer,
my best friend my dog and I.

To take in this lovely sight,
no people, no fast cars,
catch the wind in my hair
hear it sing blowing in the wind,
my mind at peace once again,
a wee bit of fresh air I declare.

Wlodzimier Kajon

TO BE TRUE

If you fool with someone's heart,
You will take them by surprise
But, if you really love them.
You'll look into their eyes

And tell them, that you need them,
And if they need you too,
And if you stay together,
Just what, you're going to do.

To be with them *forever*
And if they *love* you too
Just think about the *future*
And they'll be *there*, for you.

Forever and forever
They will *never let you down*
So please don't go too far away
But always be around.

E B Holcombe

LION CHILD

Long ago, on some auspicious day
In August, when the sun blazed
From an azure sky on this tumultuous world,
A child squalled her first defiance
Of her binding clay.

A brave spirit in a fragile shell
Of flesh, she breathed her lust for life
Through every moment of each waking day,
This child quick-silver bright by
Earthy joy impelled.

Her true heart with laughter always swathed,
Cleaving the dross and turmoil
Of our days, drawing hearts and spirits ever
Upward, towards love and hope,
Away from pain.

The lion woke and triumphed at her birth,
They shake their manes together still,
Then rest in proud content among true hearts
And happy slaves, forging a little Heaven
On this Earth.

Caroline Isherwood

I HAD A DREAM

I had a dream that people
wouldn't be so quick to judge
the failings of each other and
learn to love one another.

I had a dream that wars
would be averted as nations
learnt the meaning of compromise
and tolerance.

I had a dream that nature would
flourish freely without the artificial
interference of man, a potato
would really be a potato and
not some other form.

I had a dream that the art of
conversation would be retained
and not taken over by cyber talk
or the latest PlayStation game.

Candida Lovell-Smith

VICTORIA

Old horses pulling carriages through deep snow,
Silhouetted women,
Long black dresses and plumed hats,
Ice maidens on a plinth of air,
Victoriana delicate, serene.
Silence.
A small, thin child holding her mother's hand,
The late afternoon embracing bare trees,
Shadows on the snow
Thrown by candle lamps
From the warmth of cosy homes.
I'm standing outside, wanting in,
But the time is wrong,
One hundred years too late.
An ache in my heart to go back,
To be taken into one cosy home,
Comforted and held by this glorious scene,
For one hour, one minute, one second.
Calling me, somewhere in my mind,
The echo that belonged to my forefathers.
I reach out,
I smell the air,
A passing shadow walks over my grave,
Touching the thin child's face,
Smiling,
Leaving me here . . . alone.
Passages of passages of time,
Corridors of never-ending gentlemen,
With snow-covered shoes,
Laden with presents for children.
Great fire in the hearth,
Maids scurrying to and fro for the madam,
Curtseying and running to the scullery.

Soft flurries of snow
And the air burning her nose,
Muffs to warm her hands,
Yet she cannot taste the moment.
I will taste it for her,
Hold onto something special.
I visit her grave too, now,
I crouch and I whisper,
'I envy you,'
And she leaves me here, alone.

Jackie Bilton

ALICE

Alice was a lady's maid, a lady's maid was she,
She brushed her mistress's hair each day and poured out the tea.
She went with her on shopping trips and carried parcels three,
And when her birthday came around it was a sight to see.
There were presents everywhere from her many swains,
There was lace, fripperies, perfume,
There was bonbons and pink stockings, bracelets and gold chains.
They begged her for her hand in marriage but she did refrain,
And waited for the consort who chose to remain.

Bernadette Larry

LIFE IS SUCH A THRILLING MAGIC

Once I met a person by chance.
He and I started talking . . . meeting here and there,
Conversing, laughing, joking
That one day, we discussed even lifespan.
How long a person should live, strive and struggle.
I intruded . . . I will not like to live long,
Death is a blessing in disguise, at least for me.
He interrupted . . . how long I will like to live –
30,40, 50, 60, 70, 80, 90, 100,
And on and on so, on so far . . . forever.
Tell me please, let me know, so that
I could come to you and inform you,
Young man, this is how long you wanted to live, survive, struggle.
This is what you wanted.
I have come to let you know your time has come.
I could not respond, reciprocate to him intuitively,
Then and there, instinctively and spontaneously.
I was dumb . . . dumbfounded.
Life is such a magical web, magical wand.
We two just looked at each other, by one another silently,
Yet looking for a sensible answer, clear-cut reply,
Wondering, wandering for a sense making satisfying reason.
Although it is a simple query, it is not so clear cut.
Life the magic, eternal lust to live forever and
Ever, ever, ever and ever.
Such a magic from generation to generation,
All around the Earth, forever and for good.
Life, oh life, oh life, oh life, is it not so?
Undergo torture and tension, agony and ecstasy,
Ill, sick, still looking for cure, searching for health
And so on and on and on, encouraged and prayed by all,
Strived for by human knowledge, doctors and nurses and so forth.
I am over 60 years . . . still struggle to live, survive,
Instead of death . . .

Ghazanfer Eqbal

TRAGEDY
(Based on the Aberfan disaster)

They had always stood poised
Like ghosts in the distance
Yet they were poised
To kill
Sudden and silent
Ascending like a quiet elevator
The kids called it their temple
But this and many more were drowned
Completely, utterly, finally
But now the tiny ghosts
Are paying
Taken down
And exorcised.

Colin Jarvis

UNTITLED

For whom does the church bell toll? For thee, or thee, or me!
For many years it's tolled before . . . throughout our history.
Mourners gather round the grave to say their last goodbyes
And wonder who the next will be, whilst wiping tear-filled eyes.
There's Auntie Flo and Uncle Joe, despite their obvious wealth,
Are martyrs to their aching limbs, not in the best of health!
There's Uncle Sid, who never did 'a day's work in his life,'
And auntie Joan, who loves to moan, his downtrodden, frumpy wife!
Granny Barnes, whose crooked arms seem welded to her frame,
Mumbles curses 'neath her breath, she's always been the same!
Mouse-like Minnie with her soup-stained pinny . . . 'Could have
                                                    made an effort.'
Auntie Peg, with arthritic leg, said, looking for support.
Uncle Luke in his gaudy suit nodded to agree, till a magpie 'plopped'
Upon his head, from the old oak tree!
Chortles round the graveside are frowned upon as sin,
But the vicar simply guffawed when Agnes there broke wind!
Trying to restore order, the verger quickly spoke,
'This funeral is a sad affair, and not some kind of joke!'
'Ahem, ahem,' the vicar said, straightening up his cassock,
And proceeded with his sermon, till fat Gladys tripped over a tussock!
Over she went, all double and bent and alas, there was no stopping,
Dragging all round the graveside down, onto the wooden coffin!
'Enough is enough!' the vicar said to the gravedigger by the urn,
'For Gawd's sake fill the bloody thing in. They'll all be in there
                                                    in turn!'

Laurence Eardley

WASTE NOT, WANT NOT

Waste not, be practical and well-meaning
See to the end a provoking job
And be a want not person

Make the effort to be useful
To someone in great need
Waste not, be practical and well-meaning

Take a look around you and be a friend
To an unhappy person you know so well
And be a want not person

Rejoice in the knowledge of great happiness
That surrounds you, if you look for it
Waste not, be practical and well-meaning

Take a chance and benefit from it
The love that emerges will bring you joy
And be a want not person

Boast not of your ambitions
Keep them tightly gripped
Waste not, be practical and well-meaning
And be a want not person.

Alma Montgomery Frank

THE GORACHITE

In the times of yore
The Gorachite
Realised that his store
Of Haroonite
Was low
So he went for some more
Nearly fell to the floor
When one passed by.
Crying.

Mike Vick

FAMILIAR GROUND

Stark grey corridors, shiny floors, endless doors,
Footsteps echoing, wheelchairs clattering,
Endless streams of people questioning.
Figures hurrying to do someone's bidding,
Emergencies come by the score,
Telephones are a bore.
Machines stand to attention,
Waiting for someone who understands.
This machine is dying for want of a hand.
Floral curtain surround stiff beds,
Patients try vainly to rest weary heads.
Patience is the name of the game,
With so many problems, one could go insane.
Many people in need of care,
Yet the smiles are often there.
Poor old Bill laughs in his sleep,
Aggie complains she has lost her teeth.
Many speak as a child, nurses vary, most are kind.
Here in this place we cannot do without,
Whether we are rich or have absolutely nowt,
Waiting room's second on the right,
With a little bit of luck, you may go home tonight.

I D Welch

THE SKIER

Then more swiftly and still swifter,
Flies above the big sea water
Slaloming in and out and up and down
Leaping all the bumps if shorter.

On he speeds with graceful gestures
Flying still and yet still free
But to the world of stress returning
Yet lingers still a while in yearning.

And inevitable as the moving finger
So the seasons will move on
And the spring will come again
With summer not far beyond.

Rosemary Smith

ARRIVING (AT AGE 40)

I have arrived, so I'm told, at the beginning of life;

The train now standing at platform nine
Appears to be running out of time . . .

Will I be the same woman, mother, lover and wife
Or shed this caterpillar's skin
To sample the delights of the midday sun,
Flitting unhurriedly from one experience to another,
Unaware that I have a finite time to run?

The train now standing at platform nine
Would like to negotiate for more time . . .

To do all the things that need to be done,
Where to start? Hopefully number one!
To see the world' no - to learn to play
A musical instrument one day; today!
Or achieve an ambition without having to pay
The price of compromise.

The train now standing at platform nine
Realises that there is no time . . .

Like the present to sort things out
And begin to trust one's intuition
And enjoy this elevated position!

Sarah Allison

MOURNERS

The sun had receded and sombred her light
Water and blood poured from his side.
Earth had revolved, cracked Golgotha's rock
Friends and relations stood numb with shock.

His wounded corpse now the only thing left,
Embalmed by his nearest - of all hope bereft -
Is laid to rest in a stone-hewn tomb,
Before the rise of the Passover moon.

Had love done its work, or had evil prevailed
When to the cross Jesus was nailed?
The Father, had he abandoned His son
Or was this the moment His will was done?

No answer comes to the mourners that night,
Battered they feel by a giant tide.
As the Sabbath unfolds a moribund pall
Undreamt lies the dawn that would enthral!

Verena Ryecart

BELOW STAIRS

Where chickens clucked and a milkmaid and two ploughboys
hid in the hay barn, gobbling crusts when they should have been
working, t'wasn't much, their life, just toil and grime -
beastly objects of the squire, whose twitch kept line. Would be that he
would grind them down, servitude would see to that - before they'd
saved that silver crown, for a Sunday hat. And like those who had gone
before them, t'was expected of the poor man, hand ye over yer boys 'n'
girls, give them to a cruel world and watch them weary afore their time,
silver service, concubine. They'll know the sound of his scraping boots,
balk in the stream of his foul cheroots, know every inch of him black
and blue, his spur-of-the-moment rage on cue

The prettiest would bear his child, the bastard fruit of tainted vine, then
out she'd go with babe 'n' rags, no more desired - unwanted hag, and
on the cobbled, darkened street she'd ply her trade for rice and meat, to
feed the babe born under stairs, while carriage dames pass by and glare.
The workhouse, roof and daily fed, for those who've graced the
master's bed, a candlelight, some bread and water, no finer things for a
peasant's daughter. Grace and charm are not required and death will
come before retired, a hole beneath the barren clay, some misbegotten
friends to pray, the lasting peace, eternity - for those born into poverty—
passed over into time and tide, no mortal hand can turn aside. A stone to
mark your journey's end, where tears are all your story penned, of earth
and chattels, history . . . go you and I to purity.

Maria Daines

SILENT WORDS

Chasing rainbows in the dark
While we're in two worlds apart.
We need a pathway to glitter and shine
To join your universe to mine
Star-spangled stepping stones glimmer
Like a moonlit reflection they shimmer
A rock pool of light
In the sea of night -
Uncut diamonds in the sky
Divide your world from mine
Slicing the velvet sky.
Like bubbles bouncing,
Opal clouds pass me by.
They hide our rainbows
Dreams lost inside
As rainbow tears fall
I still stand tall
My teardrops turn to pearls
An oyster bed of forgotten words
Buried treasures of words unsaid
A silent world is lonely
Diamonds aren't a girl's best friend -
But you are mine, my rock
Alone I stand, I whisper, 'Why?'
Then snow-lace flutters gently by
Lace patterns make our pathway glow
It's melting snow, your words I hear
Your love begins to show
Such a delicate trail of crystal glitter
Glistening like snowflake litter
Together we find our opal clouds
To follow the rainbow road
Where dreams are told
And words are spoken from the heart.

Angela Sharp

THE NINTH LIFE

At least it would be of some small comfort
To know there had been so vital a cause
That would have made it almost worthwhile
For the ball of streaking fur and claws
Untidily to dispose of the ninth of its lives
In a reckless skirmish (of the one-sided type)
With my tyre, specifically the offside front,
And thereafter, the nearside rear, via I think,
Some noisy progress along the exhaust pipe.

Of course, we possibly could try to imagine
A dozen or more goals for the ill-fated beast,
Perhaps there still breathes a juicy, plump rodent
With an appointment booked for a midnight feast,
That will scurry to its hole, safe and sound,
Its whiskers a-quiver with fear, but relief
That tonight for once, it won't have to face
The fatal nemesis of needle-sharp teeth.

Or maybe we'd be better to ponder the chance
That on the other side of the road we'd find
A still ardent, but tragically unrequited lady
Expecting an encounter of the amorous kind,
Whose tail will droop in feline frustration
As she returns home to thrust herself
Against her owner's leg in desperation.

And yet, who knows, it could have been
Some deadly rival, strutting on the fence
That borders the territory of our deceased hero
Who was simply responding, with heightened sense,
To his neighbour's threat, only to find instead
Himself suddenly and sadly and thoroughly dead.

It could be some dormant jungle instinct
Was aroused at a distance by the compelling sound
Of dustbins clanging like a clarion call
Being filled with all manner of delectable morsels,
Fish-heads, meaty trimmings, leftovers and all.

Could any of these be reason enough
To discard with such abandon this mortal coil
Showing scant regard for the owner's kids
Who'll weep at the grave in the flowerbed soil?

Squashed by my wheels while in hot pursuit
Of a snack or a fight or a casual lay
Is no way for a quicksilver cat to die,

But isn't it the truth that every day
We make of our world such an awful mess

That innocent millions keep dying for less?

Dean Goodman

RECAPTURED

Inside the screaming, tortuous need
The searching, longing, heavy with pain,
Where is my refuge, where can I go?

The days go on turning dark and light
Flashing my existence, youth to age
The way still is lost, out of my touch.

A light glimmers, escapes and dies.

Respite I reach for, hand outstretched
Door of my life I open for you
My path lies before me, long and straight.

Courage leaps within my breast now
Strength to reach, hold onto my vision
I ache to become reality.
To bring me the peace I know is mine.

The light glimmers, flares and burns.

The wind rushes all around me
Sweeping my thoughts up high
The wild peace surrounds
My solace is nigh.

The grasses wave and bow low
Smiling, hiding their heads
I grow inside - tall
And laugh silently.

The flowers part for my feet
Breezes bend them aside
Communion is shared
Together we hide.

Sheila Sanderson

AUGUST

The fresh rain sings
Down the lane to rumba
A samba chuckles through my heart
I starve my anger
Under my shelter, a roof,
Looking through black covers
Dancing in the stars
Passing through smoky skies
Into cosmic thunder
Pursuing an overture of nature
Onward bound for a new today
And tomorrow and every day.

Hardeep

Whoosh!

You whip up my hair
And tease me.
Swirling round,
Mischievous,
Vibrant,
Full of life!
A reminder of
The spiritual freedom
That I aspire
To achieve for myself.

Sue Umanski

REASONS

When you see her
You secretly glow and tingle
In places you thought had died years before.
When her eyes lock into yours
You want to dance in the stillest, quietest place
And laugh from head to toe,
Yet remain tight-lipped
So not to appear too obvious.
When she speaks
Your mind roams into unnamed tomorrows
And the future we might have had
If only you had found the words,
The right combination opening a life
Of sunshine and promise.
When she turns away
The illusion is burst, that one sweet flavour
Anoints the tired air.
Next time you see her
It will be different;
The joyous struggle continues forever.

Laurence D E Calvert

THIS TIME LAST YEAR

My well-worn runners stepping across the grass,
crushing stems and silencing hoppers;
Heat haze sending shadows through the short cut stalks
sticking hard from the dry bare soil beneath.
The dog's tail waving on above the seed-heavy heads
of the hayfield swaying in the sun,
And maybe,
The fields stretch across the soft rolling hills of central Navarra -
Harvest ready yellow; stabbed and slashed here and there
where pears and plums and others ooze out of the wheat.
And we stroll inside it all.
And the blue bending above us is broken only by the brilliant ball,
Resting on the stone bronze wall,
Encasing what we just can say is good without the wind.
There's a pheasant hidden here, that would fly faster than my sight,
or show me that I am what I claim to know,
But we are one.
And soon this orb will sink,
But my days are gauged by the raven vision
gliding through the gold beside me
Who glows peace through my skin.
And the sky is to be blown apart by blue and red
Before the noise that booms below her whispers becomes a beat
that all bow to in one heaving, swaying field of joy,
After which, as the day returns we will rest,
loving languidly; our warmth dissipating balmily.
But it is all a year past and a plane-fare away.

David J O'Brien

THE EAGER BEAVER

Oh yes, 'patience is a virtue'
That's what the people say
But a certain eager beaver
Learnt this truth the hardest way
For when he heard his daddy talking
Of a dam that they should build,
With thoughts of ease and quickness
His little mind was filled.
He hurried off alone that day,
This dam to build with speed,
But he hadn't listened hard enough
For useful tips to heed.
He couldn't push the great big logs
So had to find some small.
He made mud pats and worked so hard
Asleep he soon did fall.
When he awoke, he found the dam
Built across the river.
'It's all been done, I've missed it,'
He cried out, with a shiver.
If he had waited for his dad,
Instead of being eager,
He could have helped and learnt much more
And been a wiser beaver.

Jackie Barker-Smith

TRANQUILLITY

Walking in some leafy glade,
A songbird sings on high.
I feel that spring is here at last.
My heart is full, I stop and sigh

Remembering all the carefree days,
When I was just a lad
Collecting plants and chasing rabbits.
It makes me feel quite sad.

I wonder where the time has gone
And what has progress brought?
Computers, drugs, technology.
Is this the life we sought?

Well, perhaps it is for some,
But not I fear, for me.
Give me back the peaceful life,
Let's have tranquillity.

J P Cook

LA ROUTE CÉZANNE

Aix, too, stands on the Pilgrim's Way,
another Vézélay. The narrow footpath,
heady with poppy, lavender and thyme,
leads not to Compostela
but to the brooding mass of Sainte-Victoire,
presiding, dominant, beyond Tholonet.

His footsteps stud the trottoirs of the town,
bronze scallop shells, coquilles St Paul,
marking his favourite itineraries and
coffee shops, birthplace, assorted residences,
the musty Faculty of Law, the old Cathedral,
latterly attended most assiduously.

On a green hillside, shaded by oak and sycamore,
the picture window of his upstairs studio
opens upon the world. Within, a bowl
of apples and oranges. A crucifix adorns the mantelpiece.
His *boyna* and mistral-proof, age-stiffened overcoat.
A plump, familiar, naked cherub. Grubby, in plaster.

Whether of mountain or his rock-faced wife,
himself as Shakespeare, or onions on a plate,
he strove to render pattern and depth,
to create on flatness solid form,
painting in prisms and modelling in colour,
to reconcile, like God, darkness and light.

Observe. The square-cut, quarried rocks of Baux,
the hilltop villages of the Vaucluse,
the greeny, bluish, ochre cubes of Bibemus,
Jas de Bouffan, l'Estaque and Château Noir
are piles of pigment, structured prismatically.
Provence, the canvas, bears his signature.

Norman Bissett

NUMINOUS

Perchance 'twas a dream I first crept in the grove,
Left life one dawn many miles did I rove;
I know not what land or year of discourse
Roused by soft pipings drawn to their source,
Betwixt trackless olives drunk with passion
Coherent recollection, I fail you to fashion;

At once! I beheld her softly singing
A warmth to my heart forever bringing,
There she lay sublime - an enchanting sight
Beside murmuring brook in soft moonlight,
An age I stood, in awe of that voice
Those precious seldom moments, in them rejoice;

Gently she spoke as the wind caressed sighing,
'Do not stand espying while comfort denying,
Are you not favoured to gaze upon me here,
Where no mortal has trod for a thousand years,
Once fawns and dryads danced this sacred site
Alas, dreams, love and laughter, dead to this blight;

Come sit, I was once known as Tyche,
We must hurry, our time swiftly lessens,
In you lies my hope, the purpose of your presence,
You; the last believer uncorrupted by vice
Can return to me, find me, when soon you awake,
My bond to this place, only you can break.'

Years of grey wanderings this colossal maze,
Stranger amongst strangers, moments drawn like days,
Sometimes I awake screaming out her treasured name
I turn to fellow men, unbelievers all the same.
Her memory I cherish, brightest beacon flame
I swear, I shall not fail you whilst life in me remains!

T J Shaw

PRAYER FOR THE KURSK
(To the families of the sailors written just after the sinking in 2000)

Receive the souls Lord, of a titan downed,
Give comfort to the families of sailors drowned;
Though decisive tool of political strife,
As lessened not the loss of precious life.
Beneath the waves of the sea of Barents,
Her broken hull echoes to grieving lament
But shadowing the tears of a mournful nation,
Is the dread and the fear of leaked radiation;
Too little too late is all our regrets,
Her demise as a name we call it Kismet.

W A Andrew Bray

WHILE IT'S WARM

He finds the stroke of the brush comforting.
It has a kind of rhythm of its own,
as it applies oil to canvas,
watercolour to paper.
He likes best to paint outside in summer,
with the sun on his back.
Sometimes he has to squint his eyes a little
to see what he's painting,
to get the colours, the texture right,
but it's nice.

The brush slides backwards and forwards.
Sometimes he even forgets what it is
he's actually painting.
He becomes overtaken by the motion,
the movement of his arm.
It's calming, relaxing,
as he brings it down.
The results almost pale
into insignificance by comparison,
although his studio now boasts
a fairly large collection.

The standard is mixed.
He's neither bad nor brilliant,
but good enough for his own satisfaction.
That's what counts.
That's what keeps him going
through these long months of retirement,
while his wife works on,
being almost a decade younger than him.

In an hour she'll be home.
He makes a mental note
to have her tea on in time,
but first to finish his picture,
to make the most of the weather
while it's still warm.

Andy Botterill

MY KITCHEN WINDOW

As I stand at my kitchen sink
Busily doing daily chores
I look out of my kitchen window
And marvel at the different scenes
The birds that swoop down on the lawn
Pecking up grit and pulling out worms
The neighbour's cat lurking nearby
Ready to pounce on unsuspecting prey
I bang the window and shout aloud
And the ginger tom slinks away
I'm pleased, for now I've saved a bird
But what of next time if I'm not here?
The pigeons fly around in the sky
An everyday occurrence at the same time
Blue tits land on the bird table
Pecking and dropping nuts from the net
Sparrows having a rest on the fence
Then taking bird baths in the soil
Honeysuckle climbing up the fence
Red carnations grown from cuttings
Taken from the birthday bouquet
My husband gave me the other year
These and many others are the scenes I see
When I stand and look out of my kitchen window.

Diana Daley

MYSTERY WOMAN

She appeared out of nowhere.
Not knowing her name,
I danced with this woman
With raven-black hair.
I know not where she came from,
Or where she is now,
But I'll keep on searching
Until true love is found.

A G Douco

THE DEATH OF A SEAL

'Mid the ice and snow on a sunny morn
A tiny baby seal was born.
His proud mother wiped his body dry,
Thankful the sun was shining high.

She fondled him with tender glee
And asked her neighbours,
'Does he look like me?'

As this little fellow tried to slither away,
Mother warned him not to go too far to play,
As all children do, he paid no heed,
With his friends he wandered off,
Not listening to her plead.

He had not gone far when the sound of heavy feet he heard.
What can it be? 'Tis not a bird.
Looking up with his big, beautiful eyes,
Some monster stood there by his side.

What can it be? I'm so afraid.
I wish now more heed to Mama I'd paid.

I hardly dared to breathe as I lay beneath its gaze,
As the sun glistened on the ice, in the distance was just a haze.
If Mama was looking for me,
'Twould be difficult for her to see.

The monster struck me one huge blow,
My little head rolled to and fro,
The blood poured in a pool around
As I lay there upon the ground.

Soon my mother had found me,
All the blood flowing, she could see.
Cradle me in your arms, Mother,
With your cold flipper cool my aching head.
The way that monster struck me,
I really should be dead.

But the time has come, Mama, for me to go.
No more I'll play in the ice and snow,
And suck your milk that makes me grow,
But then my blood never again will flow.

I love you Mama, and hope that you will live to see
The time when those monsters will love us seals,
As much as you love me.

Isabel Kelly

HMMM, I THINK OF YOU

Of sensual song, dancing through a bed of a thousand nights
Shimmering in the delicate embrace of moonlight.
Let the beams flood your romance, and moisten your love
For the eternity to pleasure you in a heavenly warming trance.
Open up and pull me in, for the riper fruit of your loving spin
And cloud my judgement to feed upon your breast so supple.
I want to taste you in every way, from day through night to day.
To ride you by honeymoon, will melt the sugary syrup on my spoon.
Kisses, so soft and tender, all to you from your ardent sender.

Anthony Rosato

FOREVER YOUNG

I have felt real love in my lifetime
A heart which has been broken from a father's love
Children, taken for lots of years,
So many problems, buckets of tears.
Never being the same, why can it be
A love that was, but not for me?
Being a mother I hold so dear,
Children needing me all through the years.
But a father's love we can never regain,
The hopes and dreams will probably remain.
I hold in my heart, locked up so tight,
The thought of maybe to forgive him, which is right,
But when I see what he has done
The memory will stay forever young.

Lynda Hopkinson

AFGHANISTAN

Here is a country of continual war,
Fighting for possession of territory galore
Many religious battles are fought.
The climate is hot and not very helpful
And the land is infertile, dusty and dry
Mainly due to irrigation lacking
Crops are few and far between,
Not sufficient to feed the nation.
Once governed by Taliban, the people suffered
Oppression was great and no one could gain
One mortal thing in this vast terrain!
The Royal Marines did a mighty task
To clear out the caves and weapons dumped
And perhaps to find Bin Laden if they could,
But of course, he is the artful dodger
Who could hide himself and still survive
In this wilderness - alive!
The people now are left bewildered,
Teachers are needed in desperate haste
To govern and atone,
To order in a rightful path.
This shattered country must be reborn
From the ashes left from war alone.

A E Silcock

My Own Three Predictions Of The Future

The peasant's bloody knife, great man's life depriver,
Three rulers, council great, eagle and biggest arriver;
The lands of the pagan and the Turk.
War's the fierce strife of the two states,
Both states seek each other's life with hate;
Yet all shall be destroyed by the fire,
Which does more wonders before my watery desire.
In February of year two thousand and three,
A train in Nottinghamshire will be derailed free;
It'll be caused by a vehicle wrongly used,
Going onto the railway tracks making terrorists amused.
The maiden's name shall be Louise Lucy Ferguson
Until I change it into some other one;
She will be born first as a daughter,
The only girl of twins making evil shorter.
She's of her Christian mother as Ursula predicted,
And the son of man who's restricted;
There will be two born in one day,
Doing what God says, 'Is the right way.'

Ian K A Ferguson

THE MANCHESTER GAMES

After Japan, South Korea and SW19,
Sport was over it would seem,
At least until later in the year,
When the football season resumes again here,
But Manchester had a different purpose,
To ensure the games were not surplus.

Seventy-two nations from every crevice,
Malaysia, New Zealand, St Kitts and Nevis,
Came together in England's north west
To perform among the world's best,
Netball, squash and badminton too,
Were at the Commonwealth Games 2002.

First action from the pool was swimming,
Memories of Sydney ever dimming,
For this time we secured a medal haul,
Causing the mighty Australians to fall,
After a dismal Olympics in this discipline,
The home nations proved they would not give in!

Next up of course was track and field,
Bringing in a substantial yield
Of medals - bronze, silver and gold,
On the podium a sight to behold.
Paula Radcliffe with a courageous run,
And Kelly Holmes also won,
Edwards triumphed in the triple jump
And Backley's javelin landed with a thump.

More success came in the dojo,
As Randall performed a golden throw
And with the hockey final causing debate,
For the next games I cannot wait!

Ruth Morris

SAY THE MAGIC WORD, DADDY!

Asks son of four years,
Amid spate of tears,
'Where has my cat gone, Daddy?'
'He's gone to Heaven, my little laddie!'
'Why did he go?'
'To be with other animals in Jesus' grotto!'
'How did he get knocked down on road?'
'Because he forgot to look both ways, as in Highway Code!'
'Oh! Bring him back, Daddy, say the magic word!
Please say the magic word!'

I too have lost a loved one and had to say adieu,
'Please say the magic word, Daddy, let my sunshine through.'

'Please say the magic word!
Both old and young will thank you!'

Hilary Jill Robson

THE SYSTEM

Taxed from birth, taxed to death
The day is young the sun shines high
Every day you see is with delight,
But don't worry, your number has already been picked
You will not get off so light.
You leave school
The taxman writes to you with delight.
Remember when I said you would not get off so light.
Then pay the bills, work all through the night
Step out of line, the system won't let you get off light.
Three square meals a day, then complain it's your right.
Then think, you did the crime, so do your time.
The system is at breaking point,
So then let's let the system do no crime
By categorising priority jobs.
The prison system is underfunded,
The National Health Service is too,
So let's just class these as a number one,
I wonder which services would be number two.
Start work, pay tax on your wages,
You know it's all going to a good cause.
So then, don't you think it is right
That the working man on the street should have his say
At a time when they say there is bad feeling
About the way the system is run?
The way I think is the same that many other people think,
And that is it's a time for change.
Let the one who did the crime do the time
In prison, with just the basics,
Not colour TV and computer games.
Then let's fund the NHS
And start in that order,
And let's do it now because life is getting shorter.

So let's do it, before it is too late,
Because this is the world our children will inherit,
So let's pave the way.
Let's pave the way to change
For a system that is crying to be changed.

Darren P Morrall

DANCE DIMENSION

Hairs stand on end
at the back of my neck.
A devil is armed
with a tune and a deck.
A feeling erupts
to an earth-banging beat.
Vibration cascades
in your heart, in your feet.
Light shatters darkness
in time with the sound.
Arms move like snakes
from a void in the ground.
Writhing together
we're acting as one.
Reasons for anger
and hatred are gone.
Smoke mixed with laser
like demons abroad.
Your soul is set free,
your spirit has soared.
We think of no future,
all fears left behind.
Allies in movement,
euphoric in mind.
No one is alone now,
with pity or rage.
This is my home
as I dance in the cage.

M Illsley (Cambo)

UNTITLED

Lives so far apart
And dreams,
Shimmering mist over lake, under moonlight,
Daring to believe that something more will come
In the morning
To bring them closer.

Gazing up towards the starry hosts
In the cool grey-blue of sky
An eternity is contained within their thoughts,
The memory of each
Somehow containing the mist
And making the dreams substantial.

Emma Ayling

A ROGUE AND JOSH OR ROGAN JOSH

One sultry Indian evening
Two men walked through the trees,
One of them was English, the other Japanese.
They came out in a clearing -
Across the other side
Was a massive Bengal tiger -
There was nowhere they could hide.
The Englishman was petrified
His heart began to pound
The Jap bent down, took off his shoes
Put his backpack on the ground.
He pulled out both his trainers
And quickly slipped them on,
'What are you doing?' cried the Englishman
'It's time that we had gone.'
'We can't hide from that tiger.'
'But what else can we do?'
'Wearing my trainers,' said the Jap,
'I'll run much faster than you!'

Enid Hewitt

ROWEN'S LULLABY

Little boy blue
So still on my arm
What would I not do
To keep you from harm?
I won't make you fight
For life that means pain
The fight will be cruel
If we make you remain
In this white place of light
No Heavens to gain.

Little boy blue
Midsummer's birth
We'll tuck you to sleep
In the quiet crib earth
In gown with ducks on
With mitts and socks on
Your face in the photo
Shut tight, so tiny-fine
Daisy in a dawn that's dusk
While light lasts is mine.

Katie-Ellen Hazeldine

PROGRESS 2002

What a mess, what a dreadful mess
in aid of what is called progress.
Sand and rubble everywhere,
while dust pollution fills the air.

Bollards, rails and fences too,
obstruct the workmen from our view.
Unwary folk trip arse over tup,
where paving slabs have been took up.

The old Hippodrome gone and in its place,
they're putting a clock, why, it's a disgrace.
Who wants the time in foreign parts,
when Lady Godiva has won our hearts?

For as the clock chimes, she rides her white horse,
with Peeping Tom watching over, of course.
It's enough to drive me round the bend.
Let's hope it's all worth it in the end.

Joan Jones

FORTY YEARS CELEBRATIONS

Well, Trevor, my love
Forty years of marriage, this day has begun
Wish we could share together this special day my love
But you are not here, you are in Heaven above.
If you were here it would have made us complete
So empty without, don't know if I'm on my hands or my feet.
Such great times you and I always had
All the memories and plans so sad
But on this special day I will think of you in my arms
So full of love and full of charm.
This day will not be a happy one for me
Because I won't have you in my company.
Just being without you is so hard to bear.

Anne Davey

MY BEST MISTAKE

My best mistake
I hide away
I made a choice
And wouldn't have it any other way

I left my life
And moved away
I chose my road
And am here to stay

I haven't much
I gave it away
But what I gained
Brightens every day

So my best mistake
I'm glad I made
It's the best mistake
I'll ever make.

Adam Taylor

PASSION AND PAIN

Angel of mercy, angel of light,
Guiding me through this heavenly night.
Your thoughts run through a heart that's true,
As crystal tears turn to dew.

Passion cuts deep as a thousand knives.
As we are twisted and torn through solitary lives.
With nothing gained, we hide the pain
And only emptiness remains,
Forever bound in eternal flames.

Jason Pratt

HALLAM

Have you heard of Bess
The mighty Bess of Hardwick
Who built manors as fast
As she demolished husbands?

Have you heard of Peveril of the Peak
Now alas in ruins
But still guarding Mam Tor
The trembling mountain?

Have you heard of Blue John
The cavern where Romans
Already valued and mined
This unique gem of a stone?

Have you heard of Dore
The village where Mercians decided
After so much feuding
To have peace with Northumbrians?

Have you seen in Robin Hood's country
Nestling on the flanks of hills
Lonely farms, in winter
Islands lost in desolation?

Have you met these people
Faces carved like weathered rocks
As hardy as the crops they grow
Tenderly rescuing lambs in the deep snow?

When autumn dawns on the moors
Covering them with colour
Gossamer delicately holding the morning dew
Have you see this vast sea of coral?

Have you heard of this place
That once was called Hallam
Where history and beauty
Blend so naturally?

J C Chandenier

WAR CRY

The young girl from the Sally Ann
Flits gaily round the pub
Flogging copies of the 'War Cry'
Amidst the smoke and the hub-bub.
She sees a guy who's at the bar
Looking all morose
So she goes across to where he is
And when she's standing close
She says, 'Are you a Christian?'
(She sees now he's Brahms and Liszt)
He turns and looks her up and down
'No, clear off,' he says, 'I'm an ezzisdenshallizt.'

Vince Clark

A NATURAL RACE

White horses leap the sea wall,
The finish of an epic race.
These Atlantic thoroughbreds
Have been in full rolling gallop
For hundreds of miles.
Coursing past Portugal
Glancing at Biscay
Powered on by nature's forces
Through Fizroy and Sole
Splitting to envelop Ireland.
No prancing here,
Charging on for Malin
Then my beloved West coast.
Watching them in their element,
They are manifestly beautiful.
Raising a head for a look,
Then down, boring on.
A look, then down.
Foaming manes flick toward the dark grey.
Haunting howls come on the air
As they near the line
Stopping for nothing.
They arrive,
Break and cascade upon the land
Reduced from mighty chargers
To cursed floods and splashing puddles
As hooded people fight the squalls.

Ronald Reid

I FEAR BEING SUCCESSFUL

Some success seduces the basic worth of life,
With one blow seduces divine thoughts of one's life,
Whose mind becomes thirsty for popular applause,
One who possesses money, should obey common clause.

Loss of love and faith is greedy that wishe to gain,
Self indulgence always will spread its charm in vain,
One's living should earn the blessings, that will grow kind,
We must not ever forsake a sick and divine mind.

My God, where all those with greed may flee in pain,
With their quilts come to face final Judgement again,
How ever big success with evil mind, can't shun hell,
Don't blame faith, the sovereign God, if you won't to dwell.

Upon earth life's position have a different view,
How one earns upon earth, in other world gets 's due,
All those avenging horrors can't help no one's case,
But to look those morals soul that live 'n Heaven's place.

All those that living with greed will with greed fall,
We're all destined to face Judgement after all.
That is why success is so fond of moral life,
Successful mind want to maintain the moral strife.

Caring for others, care and love will the soul save,
Delightful faith will attend sinless 'n common grave,
Who dies that way, will live full life with the echo
That is how Christ's devotees died, so long ago.

Milan Trubarac

SEASCAPE - ESCAPE

Smoky,
Spicy,
Smell of ships,
Seamen,
Sturdy,
Navy-polo'd,
Pebbles,
Smoothed
By the
Stealthy
Surge
Of the
Sea.

All these
He sees
And ill
At ease
His head defies.
Turning his eyes
Where childhood lies
The man becomes
A boy the while
A Crusoe on
His desert isle.

Coralie Campbell

HOPE

Images form in a clouded mind,
Passions are born in the depths of the heart.
Ideas evolve in the soul of mankind,
Hope is born, and this is the start.

David Morgan

EVACUEE

War wreaked havoc
and threats and fears
swarmed like summer flies.
They sent me far,
despite my tears
whilst we said goodbyes.

Desolate moors
seemed heartless, wild;
docketed, I stood
at beck and call
of fate, a child
cautioned to be good.

The house was huge,
a garden vast
and alien rolled.
The kitchen was
my place years past.
I was good as gold.

Maids were in charge;
no siblings near
with their fond support.
I was lonesome;
parents held dear
in memory caught.

Two dogs were there,
loved more than I,
sons loved even more.
Winter grew cold.
I'd said goodbye
all because of war.

Ruth Daviat

FOND MEMORIES OF LIVERPOOL

Liverpool was a homely town,
A living credit to the crown.
Each family lived in a house called home,
When our dear queen came to the throne.

Rows of houses trim and neat,
Where Uncle Joe lived down the street,
With Auntie Mag and Cousin Min,
And friendly neighbours looking in.

Not much need for welfare workers,
Gran and Gramp were willing helpers
To Mam and Dad when things got bad,
'Don't worry lass, we'll see to the lad.'

And when their heads began to reel,
They put them back on an even keel.
Not one soul was left alone,
When our dear queen came to the throne.

At night, no vandals roamed the streets,
Just the friendly bobbies on their beats
To help and comfort, do their best
And only when needed made arrests.
No vile graffiti spoilt the picture
Of the old and beautiful architecture.

The parks and gardens, large and small,
With lovely flowers and trees so tall,
Were peaceful havens where young did play
And the old did rest along the way.

The River Mersey, deep and wide, with
Ferries that took us to the other side
For a day on the sands with bucket and spade,
Clean sea water where all could wade,
Was busy with shipping that firms did own,
When our dear queen came to the throne.

Now in this year of Jubilee,
Nothing but sadness do I see.
Tower blocks here, tower blocks there,
Rising hideous in the air.

With lonely people in the sky,
Was it their wish to go so high?
The planners in their hour of greed
Forsook the people and their needs.

Alas! Now twenty-five years on
The grand communities . . . almost gone,
But I for one will not despair
Because I know in that salty air
Those gradely people will keep their cool,
Will not abandon their Liverpool.

They will do their best and always cope,
They have two cathedrals linked by a street, name Hope.
May happiness grow from the new foundations,
I wish them joy of their celebrations.

Florence Taylor

(OR) TERROR

The anger raged within his breast,
Fair put his hatred to the test,
So great a weight was this burden,
No relief would ease his pain.

He swore an oath, no rest would he find,
Until the enemy would he find, and kill.
They stole his wife and son.
The happiness was taken away that day,
They slew his father and his brothers.

Left his world, no peace again,
So great a love had this man
For his family and his clan.
He chopped the heads off the evil band,
While his hatred ran loose across the land.

A thousand days did it span; fear and terror
To every man, till none dared to ever gain
Raise a hand against this man.

M Simms

FRIENDSHIP = ATTACHMENT FROM MUTUAL ESTEEM

I looked it up in the dictionary
a cold book full of words.
Friendship, it said, meant give and take
and an estimation of worth.

'Mutual esteem',
I looked that up too and as I read
A grin slid slyly over my mouth.
The definition of 'mutual'
said: 'common, joint, shared by two.'

I closed my eyes and could almost smell
the forbidden smoke of younger days.
Do you remember Deep Purple nights and
a common joint shared by two?

Rona Laycock

JANUS FACES

Janus faces, two by two spinning
First one then the other, flipside
People made different by turns
Lit by darkness, shrouded in light
A twisted mirror, funhouse of souls
Trust nothing you hear and less you see
A face is a smudged note of the mind
Short nonsense read back to front.

James Stapleton

RAGING BULL

When your finely
crafted symmetry
no longer breathes
its fire of revenge,
and your tormented
embers are no
more than a
painful memory,
a penitent wind of
ignorance will emerge
as it blows through
empty chambers of remorse.

Let the lightning glare
from angry skies,
and storm clouds bellow
in thunderous rage,
Lest we forget
your defiant spirit
etched in blood
upon the sand!

Only through persistent protests
from fair minded people
will this barbaric activity
be finally put to rest.

Laurence Idell

VANITY

Pull in the tummy.
Do I look fat or thin?
For tomorrow is the day
Of the big weigh-in.

You know I've been good
And I've worked very hard.
I smile so sweet
As I hand in my card.
Well done then, lost two pounds!
My lips start to curve
And it's smiles all around.
I feel so proud with my head in the air.
I stick out my chest and go back to my chair.
I feel that I should have a reward.
A Weight-Watcher magazine I can afford,
It helps to build my self-esteem,
With an eating plan, that's just a dream.
So carry on, my overweight friends,
Stick it to the very end
And you will find that it does work,
Follow the plan and do not shirk!
Results: a figure to remember
And you will be a free Gold Member.

Lyn Peacock Sayers

THE HARBOUR

Beyond, those woodland hills embrace the sky.
Beneath my feet, old-fashioned cobbles lie.
Stone cottages, hotels, a village store
Look out at ships at rest along the shore.
Grey waters lap against the harbour wall
While overhead a few wheeling seagulls call.
On ochre-coloured shingle set in clay
Decrepit fishermen throughout the day
Repair their nets or talk about a past
When trawlers joined a fleet and nets were cast.

Now waves are crashing on tenacious rocks
As misty spray hangs overhead and mocks
Those fishermen who cannot put to sea.
Some unemployed are facing bankruptcy.
Sombre clouds obscure those distant hills.
They're blown by winds with fluency which shrills
Across the street and rattles window frames
As madcap Nature plays her favourite games.
At last the sea is calm and days are longer.
Boats are launched again and men are stronger.

When trippers sail with ease across the bay
Their words are set adrift along the way.
They see a harbour nestling in the arms
Of peaceful hills. What lies beneath its charms?
Vast shoals, the pride of Neptune, swim
Unversed in laws which pander to the whim
Of European quotas. Fishermen
Are angry like unharnessed beasts,
For they cannot cast their nets or see the dawn
Rise silently, they stay on land and mourn.

Nancy Reeves

HUSH, NOT A WORD

Hush, a child is starving, say not a word.
The fight is being fought by the statesmen of the world.
'Tis they must eat to sustain the fight,
the fight you say, yes the fight for right.
But what is right and what is wrong?
A starving child - where does it belong?

The starving child is a symbol of that which is wrong,
a well-fed statesman of that which is strong.
Those who are strong have pride and power.
Those who are weak starvation devour;
consumed, deprived and with hunger and pain
there is not a chance their strength to regain.

In lands far away there is food to spare;
the waste bins are full of discarded fare.
No thought for the poor, the starving, the needy -
only for self; the rich man is greedy.
Perhaps after all, it is not greed alone
but simply the fight is so far from home.

Hush! Not a word, a child is dying;
mothers and fathers are grieving and crying.

Arthur E Crisp

You

To be oblivious, to be aware
With natural beauty, of a certain flair
Independent state, intelligent mind
Individuality, an attractive find
Level-headed, definite calm
Seeing and believing there is no harm
No doubting your trust, don't have to be alert
Feeling of warmth, no feeling of hurt
Embraced with your touch, and with your kiss
Nothing more to say - spiritual bliss
Interactive brain, open and wide
Sensing my inner thoughts deep inside
Closeness, synchronised we ride
Your body moving with mine, nothing to hide
Caution and suppressed feelings are obsolete
To be relaxed again and to be complete
To be content and to be true
Is to be all that I've found in you.

Janine Ingle

PROVING THEM WRONG

Got to get a titfer tat,
Getting married, what do you think of that?
Lots of things we have to do,
Getting married, me and you,
No one gave us half a chance,
Said we would lead each other a merry dance.
Now, we have proved them wrong,
You keep whistling the wedding song.

Forty-two years have passed
And they said it wouldn't last.
I would like to do it all again, would you?
We are still on honeymoon, we two.
Opposites attract they say, it looks as if that's right,
We may not have another forty-two years ahead, but
                              then again, we might.

Maureen Arnold

RETURN TO THE GROVE

When the lovers meet,
She tells me,
Under a cavern of fuchsias, they're
Entangled in
A pool dazzle of sunny
Days of everything.
No outside.

When the lovers meet,
She tells me,
In a grotto of toys and tree ropes,
Arm in arm with
Children of their own
And everyone's. Summer
Ever inside.

Andrew Strange

WORKING DAY AND NIGHT

Oh Oxford, Oh Oxford's a wonderful sight
Everyone's working both day and by night
There's police and poets trying to express
And sexy young ladies in short mini dress
Walking up St Alddes at about half-past four
I saw a milkman delivering to the door
And at Carfax, a post girl stood alone
All about the weather she did moan.

There was a young hooker outside the bank
She said, 'Only ten pounds for a quick w**k'
Then along came a copper saying, 'Please move along,'
She said 'A free one for you,' in a poetical song
Walking up Queen Street over the plain
I went on home to write poetry again.

Eamon Healy

COUPLES

You se them on afternoon buses.
They sit in the seats marked 'disabled';
Spectacled, lined and frail.
Morning clothes changed for the shopping trip.
She wears pleated skirt and anorak,
Beige like his, over checked shirt and paisley tie.
Their shoes are almost identical,
Brown, laced and highly polished.
Nearly always, there is a stick
And they both wear leather gloves and a hat.
They belong to an age gone by
When 'for better, for worse' meant a lifetime.
Was love something that grew into a habit,
Along with the afternoon shopping
And the ritual cup of tea?

The bus stops.
They get off slowly, and walking together,
They limp away.
He holds the shopping bag,
Then, pausing, he takes her hand.
Is that habit - or love?

Margaret Wright

SEEN THROUGH THE EYES OF A CHILD

A sea of small faces, wide open eyes
Gazing in wonder at every surprise
Tales from story books, nursery rhymes too
Greetings from Pluto and Winnie the Pooh
Upon the scene Mickey Mouse and Donald Duck
Followed by Goofy and jovial Friar Tuck
Boys and girls their faces alight
As slowly the big parade came into sight
First a gigantic cake with candles high
Gasps of delight as Mary Poppins passed by
Bright gaily dressed horses prancing
Bands playing to singing and dancing
Dumbo the elephant and Peter Pan's flight
Riding Thunder Mountain to a great height
Candyfloss, ice cream and balloons galore
Thrills and excitement as never before
Many characters too many to name
As families with children to Disneyland came.

Brenda M Hadley

PLEASE UNDERSTAND . . .

I have a loud voice, and that is from choice,
I talk very serious, but I am often sick and delirious.
I say, 'Do please listen to me, try to understand and see,
Don't just pretend, try to comprehend.'
Don't read between the lines, because I talk clear and define.
People act deaf when I talk, and try to escape, how quick they walk!
To avoid confrontation and not make conversation.
That I go to a mental health day hospital is clear,
But by their faces, they show lack of interest and fear!
Why is the word 'mental' full of bad taste?
Why is it passed over, *it is no disgrace!*

It is your brain that is unhealthy, for the rich if you're wealthy,
You will pay for a private doctor who will talk things through.
So we are saying, if you're rich or royal, blood of blue,
You're allowed to have stress and worry,
But if you're working class, you must recover in a hurry!

There's definitely one rule for the rich,
Who'll call a doctor if they have an itch,
And one rule for the poor,
When after five minutes with your GP, you're quickly shown the door!

But overall, the National Health Service have treated me well,
It is Joe Bloggs, the public, who we have to educate and
                                            (each word spell,)
That being mentally ill does not always mean you're crazy!
Maybe a bit confused, and just a little hazy . . .

Janice Walpole

PASTORAL

Farmers of words
plant your seeds
to germinate
in soil made fertile
by ancient tillage
of earth kept rich
by caring sacred toil.

We cannot ignore
the past
as it lives within us
implanted in our souls
as a guiding ember
glowing in our minds

and in the darkness
of the womb of earth
our seeds seeking the light
burst into the fire
of organic life.

Time summer ripened
grain ripples
in the sun-blessed breeze . . .
a golden harvest
waiting for our scythe.

And now begins . . .
our poem.

Stephen Gyles

RAIN

Crystal droplets
Forming circlets
Kisses for
A sleeping lake.

Diamonds showering
Clusters flowering
Sparkling in
A crystal lake.

Wordless patter
Clink and shatter
Setting in
A silver lake.

Rhyming couplets
Forming circlets
Poem of
A voiceless lake.

Christala Rosina

THE PSYCHIATRIST APPOINTMENT

I'm waiting to see the psychiatrist,
he's only very young,
and it took me a long time
to get used to him,
but now my utter trust he's won.
He's always running late,
lots of patients to talk to,
help put their problems straight.
I sit looking bored at the floor,
then I notice beige trousers
walking through the door.
'Deneeez,'
'Hello Dr Mendit.'
I follow him down the corridor,
we enter his office,
there's papers all over the floor,
but I bet he knows where everything is,
of that you can be sure.
He asks me how I'm feeling,
I can be good, depressed or suicidal,
or my anorexia can be troubling me,
so we chat and talk things through.
I'm always getting into scrapes,
of one kind or another,
but he's always done his utmost to help,
and for that I'm very grateful,
of that there is no doubt.

Denyce Alexander

LETTING GO

'Where will you go in life, my child,
When the day comes and you no longer need me?'
'When I'm sixteen I'm joining the army,
a soldier I'm going to be!'

'But isn't that very dangerous?'
'Yes, but that's the life for me!'

'They're very strict; it's hard you know.'
'Oh Mummy, don't you fret,
I'm not going tomorrow
It's not for a long time yet.'

'Time will pass all too quickly, son,
it'll be here before you know it.'
'Right, I'd better get my bags packed,
where's my Action Man and teddy?
I've got to be prepared when they call me up
to show them I am ready.'

'You're right, son,
it's not for a very long time,
so come up onto my knee.
I'll tell you a story of pirates and treasure
and maybe a sailor you'll be!'

Grace McGregor

THE LIFEBOAT

Boats aren't like us they cannot weep
there's no heart to break, no loss of sleep.
They have no voice, no thought, no pride,
they just lay waiting for the tide.
Unlike the loved ones left behind
who haven't slept, only wept
with broken hearts and sad red eyes,
trying to stop the children's cries.

A boat is only as good as the man at the helm,
and a man is only as good as the boat on which he stands
and guides through the night with firm strong hands.
It was like this on the lifeboat call, when the waves were towering
thirty feet tall
with a ten knot tide out in the firth, a hurricane wind and boiling surf.

Each man knew when his phone rung, that this job must be done,
somewhere in the black night they'd have to go to save someone
they didn't know.

Down to the boathouse they all struggled, then in the lifeboat they
all huddled,
all friends and loved ones wished God speed as they set off on
their mercy deed.

The ride down the slip was swift and sure as it had been a thousand
times before
but when she lifted the coxswain knew this night of nights would test
the crew.
The walls of water fell on deck and tore at the wheelhouse as though to
wreck
but the boat was stout just like her men and they only ran off her again.

From the radio the orders were passed telling the coxswain where the
ship was last,
knowing this coast like the back of his hand, the coxswain dodged her
clear of the land.
Then one sea riding on another hit the lifeboat in a terrible smother,
man's fine work and shipwright's skill could not survive this
rolling hill.

Over she went, all battered and bent, the men inside struggled and cried,
But the cold, cruel sea never hears the cries of any poor seaman who in
it dies.

Ronald Blay

TERESA

Turmoil is my mind
Warped and faceted
Thrown into endless illusions
All played and parried against each other
Seeking the ultimate conclusions
Me and you
Could this be true
What further pain and suffering could occur
Not just for me
But also her
I think she loves me
I think it too
Her face embedded in my soul
And with her gone
An empty hole
I fill it up
With thoughts of her
And things that did occur
Between us
Please come to me
I need you now
My insecurities to the fore
Cursing myself
But wanting more
Craving emotional embrace
Wanting us to be together
So complimented
Mad and uncaring
Our sanity intact
By sharing.

Gavin Clements

LOW FIDELITY

Trust me.
Trust who? Trust you?
A Lothario whose libido
Rules his credo? Oh, no.
Your fidelity is low.
Trust me.
I know.
You see, loving me
Proves your perfidy.
It wrecks your veracity.
Your wife would agree.
Trust me.

Brenda Conn

DEATH OF A DRAGON

(For Bruce)

Enter

Three mirrors on a window ledge
guard the little dragon from the fear and dread
of the evil spirit, intent on delivering the pain
that hunts in the dark, clinging to the family's name.
But what is he doing here? Doesn't he belong
in the land of the great dream and the long
open spaces that mock the confines of this
his first prison? Rest gentle, little dragon. Wish
not for escape from the clutches of the room,
wish only to be free from those of whom
seek to destroy you before your gift is realised
and your quest is fulfilled. Rise
up, little dragon, for it is time to test those
wings and discover the path to your chosen
way. Your search will be hard and the passage arduous.
Knowledge will not come looking for you or rush
into your mind like a flooded plain,
and yet this is what you will struggle to explain
to the fields, dry as the wastelands you
have left behind.

'Be like water.'

This is the way to
Enlightenment. If you can just make the first drop fall,
then the inevitable monsoon must surely follow. But not all
of the cups will take to being filled by the water
from your source. For some it will be much later
before your wisdom is accepted. Not those that eye
you with occasional hatred or fear, but those who lie
in the dark corners of the East. Orange ellipses of fire
burn with indignation at the growing dragon's light. 'Why
must he let the *gaijin* know the secrets of our past?

What makes him think their desire will last
more than a fleeting moment for our knowledge? Test
him now. We will see how strong this dragon is and rest
his wings forever.' But the dragon has grown and he is strong
now, too strong for their warrior. The test is done.

'Be like water.'

As it crossed the vast swaths of land
bringing together the many disparate souls and
demons, so your way removes the obstacles thrust
in front of amalgamators everywhere. Just
as you say, *'Be like water.'* Then, soon as the dragon has learnt to fly
again, the world explodes in a scream of fire.

Who is this? What manner of magic is he performing?
Soon, the universe is nodding towards a burning
star, but like all raging fires, it is too soon put to sleep.
A careless breeze catches the flame and keeps
it from running free so that no corner of the earth is
held in the darkness of that most foul demon. This
fire that bellows from the mouth of the dragon is too
quickly silenced and suddenly the recesses step into
their shadows again. No matter how much the rain
douses your once indestructible flame,
your way shines through once more. Only now
you are more phoenix than dragon. Proud
as your cubist visage dances across walls,
bedazzling all in the darkness of the theatre hall.
Trapped forever in your silver cage, but still your way
leads us to the water's edge where once again you say

'Be like water'

Way.

Alex Swift

UNTITLED

We've done it before
We can do it again
Just buy a few tickets
And ease someone's pain
We all try so hard
Yet we can't do a lot
But whatever we make
Will go straight in the pot
So many are touched
By these various cancers
But what can we do
Till they find all the answers
Just keep on supporting
You know that's the best
So come to our party
And please - be my guest.

B T Bell

LASTING IMPRESSIONS

Where you've been laughing in the sunlight,
it shows.
It's funny how the skin is white,
and permanent.

Where you've been laughing in my heart,
it hurts.
It's funny, now that you've gone,
the pain lives on.

Pamela Rollin

QUESTIONS FOR MY LOVER

Lazing upon my chest and stroking his lips
I asked my lover,

'Tell me, what is the greatest thing in life?'

'The greatest thing in life, is love.'

'Go on.'

'Love is the light in mine yes
and the softness of your lids.

You, are the root of this oak
and the *gester* in my shadow.

When I sleep,
it is your breath that keeps me alive!

I just want to know you.

Let my kisses burn so deeply, that
they follow you into the chamber of your grave
and singe the soil that imprisons you!

Your feet are the pillars of this temple of worship.
Even scholars cannot fault you!

I no longer know myself,
for my heart can only beat at the sight of your beauty.

You are the message of my life,
the reason for all being.

Let me love you, until I faint from the fumes of this love,
and float into the arms of infinity.'

She paused.

'Then your love is cheap;
for your heart is weak.

I fear the wrath of your words
for you do not worship the Maker,

but the made.

Your thoughts are fearless from reproof
for you have become a pagan to my love.

Release me from such blasphemy
for I wish to play no part!

I pray to God
that in your heart,
rests a mustard seed of faith;
that will flower more than a brief season.

Do not worship me.
Your love is misplaced.
Your heart is mistaken.

Weakness, one day, will leave you
alone.

And on the day
we are judged,
when the horn will sound
and the moon turns to blood,
you may even crawl next to me, yet
leave me behind.

For although you may briefly look into my eyes,
filled with terror and regret,

you will not know me.'

Gazala Rashid

AFTERTHOUGHTS

When I go I'll take
a few of the vital things -
a few books
a few images
a few tunes
a few bottles of wine . . .
just a few of the vital things -
a blossoming flower
a sunset
a sunrise
my father's smile
my mother's embrace
the companionship of my brothers
the solace of my sister . . .
just a few of the vital things -
a few colours
a few raindrops
a few waves from the sea
a few breaths of winter . . .
just a few of the vital things -
so I'll be taking all of you.

(I hope there's a library and
a desk at which to write.
I'll write about love and you
and a few of the vital things.)

Alex Dickie

THE GUARDIAN

He stands erect
His head is held high
He watches the birds as they fly up high
All winter long he guards his domain
Until the farmer comes again
To sow his seed he'll watch them grow
And guard them from the greedy crow
His hat is battered, his coat is torn
He is really looking quite forlorn
But where he came from I just don't know
For you se, he is only an old scarecrow.

J Hannay

YEVI

Aaaah! He was the darling of the crowd,
Yevi, the masterful puppet.
Performers around him were bit players
Mere scenery was their role when Yevi took to the stage.

Centre stage was wherever Yevi graced.
And yet he was an odd idol.
Straggling, matted black hair and beard
Intertwined with plain cloth, cladding his form
Hewn from the most basic of woods.

Perhaps we were blinkered from his shape by those eyes.
My God, those eyes.
An ice-blue stare.
No, a glare.

A glare that penetrated and passed through you and left you
Stripped, bare, naked,
Even corrupted.
And once you had overcome your blushes,
Your darker side sensed a thrill and unspoken elation

And that is why they came.
Yevi's congregation swelled over and over.
Social standing was secondary if you came to worship at Yevi's altar.
But not all were faithful to his art.

Envy, greed, hatred
The catalysts driving their conscience.
Body smashed, strings torn
Yevi would perform no more.

We watched the passionless performance.
Nobody could inspire us
Not to the celestial heights
To which Yevi had raised us.

James Gibbons

THE BEAUTY OF NATURE

The beautiful trees silently grow,
Effervescently and iridescently around you,
Their leaves shine with purest green.

The sunset glows and reflects,
Above an ocean so blue,
As children call and play amid this scene.

The heart of a man
Can hold many things,
Like the look in your eye expressed
When the robin sings.
They fly south after summer,
Taking with them gold and silver memories,
Music fills the atmosphere,
As lovers hold their cherished one dear.

Simon P Jones

ME AND B4

B4 we were both lovers
T'was before you met another
We would look up to the night sky
And play out our silly wanton lie
Without caution, fear or feeling
Your abandon was my healing
Your smooth kisses fooled my mind
I responded in due kind . . .

After we were lovers
I had also many others
We would look up to the skies
I'd tell them bitter-sweetened lies
And I watched their spirits rise
And then their terrible surprise
(You know when love dies)
Before my crazy eyes

But back when we were both lovers
Yes, before you met another
When we'd look up to the skies
Play out our mad, romantic lies
You would touch me where you shouldn't
Then laugh because I couldn't
Your soft kisses soothed my mind
How Lord, was I so blind?

But then you'd had so many lovers
And since, no doubt, had many others
My whole loss was your whole gain
And when you sensed my sweetest pain
You would just do it all again
And then I woke up in the rain
To find you'd left and boarded the last train
Amused but all alone again . . .

Phil Gustard

160

UNKNOWN ALONE

Lonely I stand, lonely I wait,
The sharp ice breeze plays on my breath.
Only one sound haunts the air,
The sound of my low and deep breath
Echoing through my head, over and over.
It never stops.
The moon, bright and high
Peeps through the witch-like fingers of
The bare and lurking branches.
I still stand; I still wait.
Shadows darken my sight and the
Eyes that stare are the
Only company I have.
Distantly I hear the crashing of the waves
Churning, tumbling back and forth
Getting louder and louder as I adjust
To the slow and repetitive sound.
But as before, I still stand
I still wait.

Samuel David Hole

ROADS STRETCH

The humming teeth of the country.

Hillocks and tufts dwindle beyond scope
and dry moor grasses rise more steeply
where acquisitive sheep with stick black

legs run or stand munching on brilliant
explosions of blades of grass, the old ram
looking fiercely, its rotating jaw providing

for its future as bullocks drape their
strength, greater than any man's - the
lions of the fields, and crows, shedding

their green turds, spread large pointed wings,
hauling their feathers up to their hot black
tree top factories where indefinite bits of

living matter get crammed down the throats
of young birds who caw at the sky, the
clouds settling along the sky's edge and

the ageless blue awnings that calm thought
containing potential dawns and long quiet
evenings, when small birds panic their way

from twig to worm to tarmac and the night sun
hardly moves but spreads its pink arms over
the hill tops.

The night sky swells with light,
pouring whiteness.
Constellations are spliced together among
too many stars to name.

We drive down to the noisy town and
the tyrannical aspect of traffic lights.

David M Garnett

UNTITLED

I remember it as dreamed
Where there was no future
When we awoke
Where we dwelled
Without continuance
Alone in the whir and flicker
Of celluloid
Amongst the roar of the world
A nightmare recited
In Braille, out of darkness
To settle upon us all
Never to be purer
Your sympathy won't save us now
And neither will our love
From what we have become
So low, so low
Despised and acid
Finding beauty where we can.

Chris Lodge

LADY OF NOURISHMENT

Lady of nourishment
Hidden of excess
Sacred of power
Ruler of distinct.

Seven scorpions galling
Plotting their revenge
Dreaded of poisons
Stings in firmaments.

Moulder of mountains
Creator of the maze
Tuner of the silence
Carver of the embrace.

Lady of nourishment
Ruler of the distinct
Server of enchantment
Breather of incense.

Durlabh Singh

END OF A CHAPTER

The ocean finally reaching the shore
Dusk fading into dark
Child resting his ever-active mind
The burnt out love igniting a spark

These days are upon us
The end has begun
Finale of the performance
Bullets released from the gun

'For wisdom and experience'
The poet said to me,
'Will bring you future wiseness, you hold the golden key
Unlock the door to reveal the next path.

Sherryl Grayson

SECOND COMING

It was raining last night
when I awoke with the storming of my consciousness
and thought it was the second coming:
with flashes and crash
the sky split apart
onto my bed.

I walked in the rain from last night
today; and it was fresh and friendly
like a peach-cheeked girl:
with frosted dew-grass
the ground of the morning
soaked my feet.

Mickey Gough

THE IRRATIONAL PARADOX OF FEAR

Part One

Darkness scares some,
Not me.
I am not afraid of the unknown.
What scares me is what I know,
That is, nothing.

Why would I be afraid anyway, when I could be confident?
Why does being so confident scare me?

I tell myself to stand up and proudly be.
It makes me wonder though, what, exactly, I am being.
Is it me? Is it right for me?

How would I know?
After all, I know nothing and have no need for fear,
Thus, I am not afraid to be,
Only afraid to know what I am being.

Part Two

Laughter cheers some,
Not me.
I am indifferent to happiness.
What makes me laugh is the ridiculous,
That is, everything.

Why would I be sad anyway, when I could be happy all the time?
Why does being happy make me so indifferent?

I tell myself to relax and just be happy.
It makes me wonder though, what, exactly, I am happy about.
Is it real? Is my life that good?

How can I tell?
After all, everything is ridiculous and I have no need for sadness,
Thus, I am indifferent to being
At the thought of being happy all the time.

Adrian Webster

ICEBERG GRAVEYARD

They've come here to die.
Morbid? Maybe.
Concealed contentment is what I see,
Frozen inside,
Their tall pride
Shines from shadows of grace.

Matthew Goodyear

SUBMISSIONS INVITED
SOMETHING FOR EVERYONE

POETRY NOW 2003 - Any subject,
any style, any time.

WOMENSWORDS 2003 - Strictly women,
have your say the female way!

STRONGWORDS 2003 - Warning!
Age restriction, must be between 16-24,
opinionated and have strong views.
(Not for the faint-hearted)

All poems no longer than 30 lines.
Always welcome! No fee!
Cash Prizes to be won!

Mark your envelope (eg *Poetry Now*) *2003*
Send to:
Forward Press Ltd
Remus House, Coltsfoot Drive,
Peterborough, PE2 9JX

OVER £10,000 POETRY PRIZES
TO BE WON!

Judging will take place in October 2003